HOW TO STOP FLOG

HOW TO
STOP FLOGGING
A DEAD HORSE

The Business Owner's Guide
To Creating Happy Endings

ALISON CLARK

First Published In Great Britain 2006
by www.BookShaker.com

Typeset in Trebuchet

To Lorna Ramsay who first encouraged me to write this book

CONTENTS

ACKNOWLEDGEMENTS

Thanks to all who contributed; your experience was used whether or not your name appears in the text!

- Amethyst Management Consulting Ltd: jas@amethyst-consulting.com
- Chris and Jan Attkins: www.vision-unlimited.co.uk
- Churchmouse Cheeses: www.churchmousecheeses.com
- Denise Barker Disability Consultancy: www.warriorqueen.co.uk
- Gentle Leadership Ltd: www.gentleleadership.com
- HG Training and Consultancy: info@hgtraining.co.uk
- Jackson Mills Associates: www.jacksonmills.com
- Jilly Shaul, The Naked Coach: www.thenakedcoach.com
- John Driscoll, Dove Nest Group: www.dovenest.co.uk
- Kate French Associates: www.katefrench.com
- Mandy Evans Ewing of Ananda: www.ananda.uk.com
- Mary Snowman of Good InTENTions: www.indian-tents.co.uk
- Nikki Wyatt: www.spiritoftransformation.com
- Phil Olley Consulting: www.PhilOlley.com
- Susan Mackay of Healing Pathways: +44 01700 502139
- Wilma Taggart: oliva.orange@terra.es

Some businesses who kindly contributed their experiences have chosen to remain anonymous. My thanks to you, you know who you are!

FOREWORD

The relevance and timeliness of this book are evident in the increasing number of choices we face whether in business or in our personal lives. When selecting a toothbrush or a brand of washing powder from a supermarket shelf becomes a ten minute crisis of indecision, how much more difficult is it for us to make important moves which will shape our futures in a complex and perplexing world?

Alison Clark has written a very readable and instructive short book on the art of ending things gracefully and tackling the process of change. She knows the value of being succinct, an important skill when the name of your business is Words in Action, and has written a book which can be read quickly and kept handy for an instant refresher. There are plenty of real-life stories to maintain interest and practical exercises help the reader progress. There is a really useful chapter on techniques for ending conversations, closing sales, finishing business relationships and even sacking clients.

Alison has written this book primarily for small business owners and people contemplating self-employment. Increasing the number of successful start-ups and growing businesses is a vital part of Scotland's economic future. But we must be careful not to let the theory and statistics of policy-making obscure the quiet courage and terrible optimism of the people who dare to make their dreams reality. A publication like this that can help them to understand and deal with their challenges, show them that they are not alone and help them to be successful is to be welcomed with open arms.

Alison works with words to make her living, helping people to understand and express their thoughts and feelings. The proper and sympathetic use of language improves our relationships, how we live and how we do business. Every day we are faced with the manipulation of language to conceal, to control or to mislead. Straight talking and clear thinking are to be valued and fought for in business and in private and public life. I commend both Alison Clark and her book, and hope it is the first of many.

Agnes Samuel

Chief Executive, The GO Group, www.go.uk.com

INTRODUCTION

When we have invested time and energy in an enterprise, it's a big challenge to let it go and move on. How can we abandon a project in which we've invested so much? It can be even harder if family and friends encourage us to hang in:

"Don't throw in the towel. Give it one more shot."

I'm not knocking perseverance. Sir Francis Drake said that it was not the beginning of a project that counted but seeing it through to the end. There are however, times when we need to know when to let go.

"We teach best what we most need to learn."

I don't know who first said it but I've certainly found it to be true. When I'm seeking to support or advise someone else, I often find that what I'm telling them is exactly the advice or the action I most need to take myself. And it can involve an extra 'stretch' of honesty to admit it!

The idea for this book arose at a gathering of personal and business coaches. As part of our mutual introductions, we were asked to say what our particular area of expertise was. To my surprise, I heard myself saying "I'm an expert in endings." I had not planned to say this nor had I ever previously described myself in such a way. I went on to explain somewhat ruefully that life seemed to have presented me with a number of situations which involved winding up, taking leave, or rounding off. No sooner had I joined a group than it turned out to be on the brink of folding. I would publish a piece only to find that it appeared in a magazine's final issue. My personal life has featured its share of partings.

These experiences have no doubt been the result of choices I have made. I could be described as a serial re-inventor of myself. I have had several careers and moved house many times. So I have learned a lot of lessons as you can imagine.

Eight years ago I gave up teaching to start my own business. Over twenty years ago, I co-founded and helped run a small retreat house and wound that up five years later. I have chaired meetings of organisations working their way through the process of ending. I have coached people who started new businesses and people who wanted to make major career changes.

On the personal side, my own experiences have enabled me to support friends and family when they have needed to move on. But that's for another book! This one focuses on the challenges that face the owners of small businesses and those of you who are keen to strike out on your own as self-employed.

There's plenty of advice around on starting up and running a business. What I'm exploring here is how we can move on when we feel stuck. As we know, a new beginning entails an ending and a happy ending is a much better basis for moving on than an ending that's messy and miserable. But if you find it hard to let go of an existing commitment or relinquish a cherished project, even when you know in your heart that the life has gone out of it, then this book will help. It will stop you from flogging that dead horse and help you find a new one.

CHAPTER 1

HOW TO STOP FLOGGING A DEAD HORSE

WHAT DOES 'ENDING' MEAN TO YOU?

I'll begin by inviting you to consider what the word 'ending' means to you. I focus on this because your business is an extension of yourself. However much we separate the business from our personal life – and it's important for our health to do that – the business expresses aspects of our own personality. It cannot be otherwise. It also reflects aspects of the business culture we are part of.

In America today, many people look positively on situations which in the UK would be regarded as business failure. If something hasn't worked, the attitude goes, let's find out why and try again. Thomas Edison is quoted as saying:

"If I find 10,000 ways something won't work, I haven't failed. I am not discouraged, because every wrong attempt discarded is often a step forward.."

This side of the pond, we still struggle with the stigma of 'getting it wrong'. So when we think of a word like 'ending', the thoughts associated may run something like this:

4

"I made the wrong choice", "I messed up", "I shouldn't have taken that tack", "I should have known".

On the other hand, there are those who blame circumstances – the tax system, red tape – or they blame other people – *"you can't get the staff!"*

Neither attitude is helpful. It is not productive to feel either a failure or a victim. It is much more energising to take responsibility for our own destiny. What does it mean to take responsibility? It means that we view our situation as objectively as we can, weigh up what elements we can change and act on these by reviewing the options and making a choice. What we're talking about here are habits of thinking, the grooves along which our minds regularly run. In order to change these habits, we need first to be aware of them.

So what do you immediately think of when you read the word 'ending'? Write down as many thoughts as you can in 15 seconds.

If your list includes negatives – *dead end, road block, loss,* or even *death* I invite you to rethink the meaning of 'endings'.

Consider the classic ending of the fairy story: ...*and they all lived happily ever after*.

Or the famous concluding words of 'Gone with the Wind'...*tomorrow is another day*. Both of these are future-focussed; the endings are new beginnings.

If you associate an ending with change and opportunity, then you will respond with ease when a new start beckons. But if the words you wrote in the box include some negatives then try the following exercise.

THE OPEN ROAD

Have you ever been travelling along a road or path and found it blocked by a fallen tree or a landslide? If you have, you must have found a way out or been rescued or you'd still be sitting there instead of reading this.

So how did you cope? Did you climb around it, clear it away, go back the way you came? Did you make camp until the lifting gear arrived to move the obstacle? Were you helicoptered out?

Whatever action you took, it was not The End. It may have changed the course of the day or the course of the journey but you have survived to tell the tale.

A few years ago, dramatic storms caused such sudden and severe flooding in Edinburgh that trains were suspended and what few buses could get through were packed. I was stranded in the city only 40 miles from Glasgow where I was booked to deliver a day's training the following morning. I managed to secure for the night one of the last affordable beds in the city and made my way there through the rain.

Even if the trains should be running in the morning, I would have no time to get to the office to pick up course material and equipment so I would have to turn up in the clothes I was wearing and with only a lipstick as a gesture towards makeup. I think I succeeded in buying a toothbrush and as my accommodation was in a university hall of residence, I reckoned there must be laundry facilities. So I washed my underwear and ironed it dry and collapsed into bed. I did succeed in catching a morning train, and arrived in Glasgow in time to deliver the course without benefit of visual aids or attempt at glamour. At least I knew I was wearing clean knickers!

Take a moment to think of an obstacle in your life which seemed to bring you to a complete halt. It can be personal or work-related but choose something specific rather than a general difficulty. In the box below, note down what it was and what you did about it.

To what extent were you responsible for redirecting events? List the things you thought and did and the decisions you took.

These are resources that you possess and that you have brought to bear on previous challenges. Bringing them into your present awareness will give you confidence about coping with apparent dead ends.

In the box below write down how you can use these skills and resources to open up the way ahead. For example:

I will have the confidence to ring up someone who may be able to help me.

I will remind myself that I am good at getting people on side and negotiating a solution.

CHAPTER 2

OVERCOMING DEAD HORSE PHOBIA

FACING THE NEED FOR CHANGE

Perhaps you are afraid to look closely in case you discover that your horse is dead. Our ability to avoid or deny unwelcome information is astonishing. I know people who throw unopened bills in the bin. They're not stupid; at some level they know that this road leads to disaster but the challenge of facing the bad news and the bank manager is too much for them. If you are verging on the 'money phobic', there are some useful contacts in the resources section.

In the same way, we can know that a project or a way of doing things has come to the end of its shelf life but we muddle along rather than face the upheaval that change brings.

Human beings are innately conservative. This ensures a certain degree of stability in society. But stability can become stagnation unless some of us embrace, and even agitate for, new ways of doing things. You might expect entrepreneurs to like change but that doesn't mean that it's easy. Even the most adventurous can get stuck sometimes.

Kate worked in marketing and project management and retrained as a coach when she finally decided to make the big change: *"it took a passing comment from my partner about this 'being the fifth time that I was going to do something different' to spur me into action."*

Do you know what you want to do and can't seem to get in gear? The natural resistance that comes before a big change has been called 'inertia mode'. If a physical body has established a momentum, we need to act on it doubly hard to move it in a different direction. So when we want to make a big change, we need to make an extra effort.

When that effort includes ending a project or winding up a business, it is easy to find reasons for continuing. That's why we need to overcome our 'dead horse phobia' and take a good look at the excuses we give for avoiding the issue.

CHALLENGING THOSE EXCUSES

Do you recognise any of these?

We're nearly there – it would be a shame to give up now!	
I'm sure we could be up and running in a month if we just put in another 10 grand	

How will I face all these people who've supported me; they'll be so disappointed.	
It's a waste of all the resources that have been put into it.	
It was *such* a good idea!	
Who'll do it if we don't?	
It's an admission of failure...	
I can't give up the day job –it's my safety net.	

If you were advising someone else, you would be able to provide a counter argument to these. Complete the boxes now before turning the page to read my suggestions.

The numbers below refer you to the relevant sections of this book.

We're nearly there – it would be a shame to give up now!	*How many times have you said this?* *2 & 3*
I'm sure we could be up and running in a month if we just put in another 10 grand	*Know when to cut your losses in time and money* *2 & 3*
How will I face all these people who've supported me; they'll be so disappointed.	*Tough* *First aid kit*
It's a waste of all the resources that have been put into it.	*Recycle them* *6*
It was *such* a good idea!	*Give it away* *Implement it another way, another time* *6*

Who'll do it if we don't?	*You're not indispensable* *2, 4 & 5*
It's an admission of failure...	*Not necessarily* *2 & First Aid Kit*
I can't give up the day job –it's my safety net.	*But it's tying you up* *4 & 5*

Easy to say? Let's look at these in more detail.

It's an admission of failure

If I give up it will mean admitting I made the wrong choice, that I couldn't cope, or that I should never have embarked on the project in the first place. I dread the voices that will say, *"I told you so."*

It's especially hard to let go of a project that you've undertaken in the face of opposition. Family and friends warned you that it would all end in tears. To admit that the game's over, feels like agreeing that they were right. And we all have our pride.

But let's suppose that they were 'right' in the sense that they foresaw challenges that you were not equipped to deal with at the time. You *did* bite off more than you could chew, you *were* undercapitalised. But now you possess that knowledge for yourself because you have experienced it. You have tested the reality of your choices, and so you are better informed for making future decisions. Your nearest and dearest will probably be more understanding than you fear but even if they should go in for, "you can't say we didn't warn you", you don't have to buy it. You've learned how to do things differently next time! Apply the First Aid Kit (later in this chapter) if the process is painful.

The alternative scenario is that others may be wrong. You pulled it off or you solved the financial conundrum facing your business. It would be an understandable pleasure to prove the headshakers wrong by sticking with the successful project even when it's time to move on to a new challenge. But even success can be a trap so remember that nothing stays the same. Unless we take positive steps for continuous improvement, entropy will set in and you will lose ground.

Moving back to the top of the list, let's look at the first two...

'We're nearly there' and 'If we just put in...

These are very seductive because underlying them is the thought of time and money already spent. Many a project goes ahead when it shouldn't because no one dares cancel it. But better to cut our losses than plough on doing the wrong thing.

SIGNPOSTS

It used to be thought that changing jobs every other year was a sign of unreliability. Now we can expect an average of 5 career changes in our working lives – and that's careers, not jobs. Industries come and go, businesses are born and die, so serial employment moves are inevitable. It's also true that we place a different emphasis on some of the traditional values.

Today, being adaptable is prized above being dependable. This book seeks to support you to hone your skills for change. But when does moving on become avoidance? How can we be sure that we're not running away from a reality we don't want to face?

To be at the mercy of the latest fad, be it a network marketing scheme or the latest software is to be a passenger rather than to be in the driving seat. Change that takes us closer to where we want to be, results from answering the prompting of our authentic desires.

Signposts to indicate that it's time to consider a change:

- You repeatedly find yourself back at the same point, encountering the same problems.

- You become aware of a gut feeling you've been trying to ignore!

In chapter 3 I'll show you how to recognise the moment when you need to stop flogging that horse. To support you with these challenging decisions, check out the contents of the First Aid Kit.

FIRST AID KIT

This kit contains tools for coping with the fear of disappointing friends, family and associates. With any luck, they will respect and support your decisions but if you are being held back by fear of how they may respond, use the contents.

Warning: this is a DIY kit. You will need to apply it to yourself using the following:

- Honesty
- Clarity
- Determination

Item 1 ~ Declaration of Rights

It is likely that you are suffering from a duty overdose. The Declaration of Rights is the antidote. Remind yourself of the following:

- I have the right to set my own priorities
- I have the right to make my own decisions
- I have the right to have those decisions respected
- I have the right to make mistakes
  (and learn from them)
- I have the right to change my mind

To fulfil your duty to others, treat them responsibly by

- Keeping them informed
- Closing out appropriately any outstanding business

Item 2 ~ Support

Seek your support from those who have *your* best interests at heart. People with a high investment in what you're doing now are less likely to be objective. Take account of their viewpoint but be aware that it's a partial picture.

Item 3 ~ The Reality Challenge

Offer the handwringers the reality challenge by asking how much time and energy they can spare for the project they say they wish you to continue. Perhaps they would like to take it on by investing time and/or money in your business?

Apply this challenge clearly and neutrally without aggression or sarcasm, as in, *"Well, you take over and see how you like it!"* It is a real option after all. It may be that you *can* hand over to someone else in a way that allows the enterprise to continue

Item 4 ~ Strengthen yourself

You need to be on form if you are to resist even well-intentioned pressure from others. So, top up the self-care by:

- Getting enough rest and exercise
- Eating a well-balanced diet
- Drinking plenty of water
- Enjoying some time out to relax
- Using stress management strategies
- Practising positive thinking

Item 5 ~ Rewards

Prepare a treat for yourself to enjoy as a reward for handling a challenging conversation or hostile response. It could be a night out on the town or a soak in the bath – whatever does it for you. And make sure that you reward your supporters – a word of appreciation may be all that's needed!

Use this kit and:

- You may experience an increase in self – confidence
- New opportunities may present themselves
- You'll significantly increase your risk of success

CHAPTER 3

HOW TO TELL IF THE HORSE IS DEAD

CHECKING FOR VITAL SIGNS

Does it keep stopping to graze? Is it refusing fences? Has it collapsed altogether?

It may be ill, exhausted, undernourished, pining or pissed off. Check for vital signs. If there's still a pulse, ask what seems to be the trouble.

Maybe it needs a break. Put it out to grass for a while then assess the situation by asking two questions:

1. Is the creature lively and raring to go?
2. How have you been managing without it?

You can see where this is heading I'm sure. It would be cruel to flog it into action if it's clearly not interested in being saddled up for a canter. If it has heaved the final sigh of relief and departed to the great meadow in the sky, you've got your answer. If in the interim, you begged or borrowed another horse, bought a moped or a tractor, you have demonstrated that you can manage without it. Perhaps change is beckoning.

I guess I'm an example of that. When I gave up teaching to launch my business, a number of factors had come together. One of these was that I had an enforced spell 'out to grass' during a period of poor health. Recovering from elective surgery, I reviewed my options. I had always cherished a vision of working freelance as a writer and presenter and I had been offered a contract that would have been difficult to fulfil while continuing in teaching. Could this be the springboard for embarking on my new life?

I loved teaching in spite of and because of its challenges, but I was ready for a change. The practical arguments made sense: if I wanted to do a good job on the contract, I needed to give it my full attention. But the clincher was not in the realm of reason but in the realm of feeling. When I contemplated returning to the classroom, I could feel my energy levels sink to the floor. Mad though it seemed to become self employed while still convalescent, I just knew that my recovery would be jeopardised if I forced myself back into the old mould.

Most of us make a move when the bother of staying where we are becomes greater than the bother of changing. There are snags however in delaying change until our situation becomes quite unbearable.

If you wait until the horse collapses under you before you think about replacing it, you won't even get to the stables to choose another. When you finally arrive, having had to walk, you'll have to take whatever's available even supposing you have the money to pay for it...and perhaps another horse is not the answer. It is, after all, the same solution as before and unless you manage things differently this time, you'll be back at the stables again with another corpse somewhere out on the road.

When Kate was made redundant, she "didn't want to look for the same ol' jobs again." As we saw, it was Kate's partner whose passing comment made her realise that she'd been putting off the big decision. This prompted her to tackle it...

"...knowing the costs to you mentally and physically for not making change is important. Also realising that when you are unhappy those around you also become unhappy. So deciding to 'stop flogging a dead horse' for me was when I took control of my destiny and began to explore what actually I could do instead of carrying on with what I've always done."

LISTEN TO YOUR SELF

How do you know when it's time to go? Listen to that inner voice you've been ignoring and listen to your body.

Interestingly, Kate used a similar form of words without any prompting from me. In response to the question about what made it possible to let go and move on, she replied, *"Trusting my body and instinct that it was time for something new."*

So ask yourself how you're feeling. Is everything an effort?

Sure some things need to be worked at. Not many of us glow with delight as we clean the oven, or complete our tax return. It's when we need to brace ourselves for almost every task, or when Monday approaches with all the allure of a trip to the undertakers that we need to be concerned.

A piece of advice I have found useful is to go through your diary for the week and mark activities according to whether they are 'heart' or 'head'. This is not anti-intellectual – you may be an astrophysicist doing complicated calculations and still be engaged at the heart level. It's not about the nature of the task but about the nature of your involvement with it.

Think of the tax return: your head tells you it must be done – is your heart leaping with excitement? Not unless you're an accountant and in the right job! Our language reveals that we know this: "his heart's not in it." So go through the week and mark these activities by drawing a heart or a cauliflower (unless you can draw a brain). Now see what the balance looks like. If in a typical week, there are too many cauliflowers and too few hearts then it's time for a change.

ATTITUDES TO TIREDNESS

Are you aware of being tired or lethargic or do you:

- Ignore tiredness
- Accept tiredness
- Believe that people who are fresh and rested can't be working hard enough

If we simply ignore feelings of fatigue, and struggle on, our bodies will adapt at least for a time. Human beings are remarkably resilient. But if the pressure goes on for too long, our physical or mental health may suffer. Our relationships with others almost certainly will when we snap at them or withdraw altogether with no energy left for social contact. Or, if maintaining relationships and pleasing people is a high priority for us, we will be the one to suffer as we put on the *smile that we keep in the jar by the door*.

The trouble is that we often don't know that this is happening. It's a gradual process and our ability to cope dulls our awareness of how we're feeling. If you've ever suffered from a bad bout of flu, you'll know what it is to realise one day – it could be weeks or even months later – that you're finally feeling yourself again. In the preceding weeks, you've felt well enough to get back to work. Now though, when your old energy and zest for life is back, you realise that you've not been running on all cylinders.

One of my hobbyhorses is the short holiday habit. I love short breaks and I take them when I can but there is no substitute for a proper holiday, when you remove your watch, switch off the phone and leave the laptop behind. The ideal length in my view is 3 weeks, 1 to wind down, 1 to have a ball and 1 to wind up again. A bit of a pipe dream!

But you get my point. We tend not to stop long enough to notice how much we need a break. So our bodies learn the new default position of being permanently tired. Research indicates that most UK adults are sleep-deprived which means that the essential physiological renewal we need does not take place. Then again, maybe it's not more sleep you need but more fun. When did you last have a good laugh?

We all go through times when life places extra demands on us, be it a house move, an illness in the family or a particularly busy time at work. We just have to keep going. While there are occasions when that is true it's worth checking whether it is *really* true in every case.

People often say things like, "Well, you've just got to get on with it." But think about a time when you were out of action while everyone else had to do the things you had planned to do. This could be a time when you broke your ankle and had to sit with your leg in plaster, or a time when your car broke down and you didn't make it to an important appointment. Obviously we don't want to let people down but there are times when we are forcibly prevented from doing things. Indeed it could be said that at some level we bring such events about because it's our only way to stop ourselves. It would have seemed unthinkable to pull out of the meeting or leave essential tasks to others. And yet, when we just can't be there, the world goes on without us.

It is harder for us to make the assertive decision to say "no", to ask for help, to cancel an event when we don't have a 'circumstance beyond our control' to blame. Wouldn't it be good though to take responsibility for our health and welfare by stopping ourselves before we break a limb or drive into a hedge?

When we work for ourselves, it's particularly important to honour commitments but if we have established a reputation for reliability and quality service, we are not likely to lose that because of one unfortunate occurrence.

Take a Break

Running a business makes one particularly vulnerable to the temptation to keep going. If you don't work, you don't pay the bills. Some business owners, especially in the early stages, work 24/7 and don't get a break at all for the first few years. Even if it seems unavoidable at the start, begin to build in time off as soon as it's possible.

Otherwise working non-stop will become a habit that you can't break. It's been said, that if you do what you really love, you'll never have to do another day's work. If we define 'work' as doing unwelcome things for money, then yes, that's true. But even if you are passionate about what you do and the hours just melt away, you still need a break from it to recharge your batteries and allow fresh ideas and energy to emerge.

How are you going to make strategic decisions about the future direction of your business if you don't take time to step back and think about it?

Have you resisted taking on more staff? Are you so attached to your business idea that you are unwilling to modify or adapt it? It's easy to fall into the trap of offering what you *think* your customers need instead of providing what they want.

A 'gap in the market' is not a matter of what they ought to buy if they knew what was good for them! It's about seeing where an actual demand is not being met. And yes, it can be about creating a demand for something nobody knew they wanted but that may not work right away. Perhaps, if you build a loyal clientele, they will in time be attracted to buy your dream product. Meantime, don't flog a dead horse.

Sometimes, external circumstances affect your business. Perhaps you have served a local area that's now changing. Perhaps it's easier for your customers to buy online. Services that you offered may now be provided in-house. New regulations may impact on what you do. If we do take time to look over the parapet, we may see change coming and prepare to adapt. Sometimes it takes us unawares or there's no way we could have known. Once you get the picture, don't waste time and energy bemoaning the fact.

Assess whether this horse just needs a rest or whether it's had it. It may be that your idea will come back into fashion. It may be that given time you can compete with the innovators and sell your products online too. Perhaps the change in your environment will bring new opportunities.

If you can do so without harm to the rest of the business then put that activity on the back burner. But if it's costing you time, money and energy for very little return, it's time to let go entirely and focus on your other business activities.

The new plan needs to have the opposite effect of that clutch in the gut. It needs to expand and lighten you, to allow you to feel that you've discovered yourself, perhaps even for the first time. A tall order? Maybe, but if you've ever experienced this, you'll know that nothing else will do.

Wilma set up her own training consultancy because she wanted to deliver services to her own standards and in her own way. She vividly remembers, *"the daily feeling of dread about going into my old job prior to resigning"* and *"the feeling of elation when I finally did get out!"*

The day *I* decided to leave, I raced to the nearest wine shop, bought a bottle of bubbly and hailed a taxi home.

The rider not the horse

Could it be the rider that's the problem and not the horse? Some of us like change and cope well if it comes along; some actively seek it out. Others seem completely unable to deal with it, going to great lengths to avoid whatever needs confronting in their lives.

Stuff happens, as they say, and some of it is outside our influence. But to exert influence over what *is* within our control we need to have a degree of understanding of our own processes.

When we find ourselves facing the same difficulties all over again, it may be that it's not the frying pan or the fire that's the problem, but the things we're throwing in!

"I moved to another department and it was the same old story - taken for granted as usual!" Perhaps she needs to learn to say no or to negotiate her workload.

"I still get left to do everything just like before." Maybe he needs to learn to delegate.

"Nobody ever tells me anything." So, ask!

The place to look for clues is the repeating pattern. When we find ourselves complaining about the same things, struggling with the same sorts of people - the bully, the slacker, the gossip etc - it may be useful to learn how we can *deal with* the challenges instead of walking away from them.

We'll feel a whole lot better - and be more productive - if we're willing to look at our contribution to an unsatisfactory situation and to take responsibility for it. A friend of mine has a question, which she regularly used to ask me...

"Come on, Alison, what's the learning for you in this?"

I could have been tempted to tell her to shut up if it hadn't been for the fact that I knew she was subjecting herself to the same rigorous process. It's enormously helpful because it salvages something out of the direst scenarios and gives us a chance to grow and change with more awareness and so with more options in any situation.

If we stay where we are, we operate more skilfully and more insightfully. If we change jobs or branch out on our own, we take our developing skills and awareness with us rather than simply repeating old mistakes.

I had a client once who had lost confidence in the leadership of his organisation and felt that his contribution was being sidelined.

He had an option to resign from his job and join in partnership with a friend who had already set up on his own. They had exciting ideas and believed they could complement each other well. The friend was urging my client to jump and he had been hovering on the edge of a decision for some time.

I encouraged him to take a hard look at himself, his present position and the opportunity presented to him. He had a family to educate through college and university, a standard of living to maintain – and a wife who was being driven crazy by his vacillations!

He decided to stay with his company, partly as a result of the time he had spent reflecting on the matter and partly because changes in the management structure gave him more influence and consequently more satisfaction. He was much happier because he had taken time to think through the options and so was able to stay without being trammelled by feelings of dissatisfaction and indecision. Perhaps in the future he may decide the time is right to branch out, who knows?

It's possible that after resting the horse and exploring the terrain, you may decide to saddle up again and carry on.

Many decisions are made for a complex of reasons and are not a straightforward *either/or*. We live in a world of such uncertainty and such constant change that it's understandable that we should look for some fixed points. The more anxious we are to make the 'right' decision, the more difficult it can be actually to decide.

We can only make the best decision we can with the information we have available at the time. Having done that, we can commit to the decision without looking over our shoulder at what might-have-been. If another opportunity comes along in the future, we'll be in a good position to evaluate it.

Wilma: ... *I usually struggle with decisions and then later on wonder why it took so long and what would be different if I had made the move sooner.*

There are always lessons to be learned and I hope past experience will make any future decision-making easier. ...No matter the path we choose, there will be other options later on, no matter how we view the decisions taken...

STUFF HAPPENS

Sometimes life doesn't wait for us to conduct a review of our priorities. John and Julie lived through a series of dramatic life events. As Julie succinctly puts it:

"My dad had died suddenly, I broke my leg before our wedding 6 weeks later, my gran died 4 weeks after our wedding and both of us thought 'Life's too bloody short for this!'"

Her husband John had worked for 10 years as a financial adviser, a job he didn't much like. Julie had been running her own business for some years as a conference venue finder. They agreed that they wanted, *"to live in the country in a small town, to be involved in the local community and to have more time to ourselves, doing the things we enjoy."*

So they sold their Manchester home and moved north to a small market town where they opened a specialist cheese shop. John adores food and loves talking to people. Julie can run her business from anywhere and also brought her business acumen to the new venture. The business is now 3 years old and they employ 8 people. They work much harder, they say, but they spend more time together.

When you visit the shop, their involvement in the local area is obvious. Not only do they source local produce as much as possible but they run events which, while providing a showcase for their own business, draw in a range of other people and make a contribution to the life of the community.

Of course, it's not all plain sailing. New ventures bring new challenges. Julie and John worked hard on a business plan, *"to prove to ourselves, more than anyone else, that the new business was going to be a success."* But there were challenges they could not have predicted and others which, though they foresaw them, had an impact they could only fully understand once they lived through them.

Recruiting for example. *"Staff is always a problem in a small town and we have to work hard to maintain a balance between keeping staff happy and making sure we have enough staff in on each day."*

Spending more time together is one of the benefits but that too needs careful management. If you run a 24/7 business, time off together depends on being able to find and delegate to staff. That doesn't happen overnight. And when you do take a break, how do you avoid talking shop on the beach?

It's an ongoing process that needs open communication and time devoted to reflecting on the balance between business and personal life.

LETTING A GOOD HORSE GO

It may be that you have a perfectly good horse but it's not the one for you. So sell it or give it away.

Selling a profitable business is an obvious example. In the small town near where I live, a successful café owner was well known for good catering and friendly service. He sold the business as a going concern because he wanted to return to an earlier interest in photography. He has set up a studio and is already doing well. The new proprietors of the café are continuing its tradition of good food at affordable prices. A happy ending and a new beginning all round.

But it does take courage to give up a successful enterprise, to judge when the time is right and to face the necessary legal and logistical processes. It's tempting to take the easy option and stay put but the status quo is just that – how things are right now. The present may deteriorate into an uncertain future if we don't take an opportunity that beckons.

GIVE THE IDEA AWAY

Just because an idea is brilliant, it doesn't mean *you* have to be the one to carry it out. If you've experienced the flash of inspiration and the excitement of dreaming up how it could all work, it's understandable that you should want to bring the project to fruition. Partly for the satisfaction and partly – we're only human after all – to gain the credit for your genius!

I fell in love with an architectural gem of a building which was up for sale. Set in a beautiful location, I could see it as a centre for holistic therapies with treatment rooms and space for group activities. Local practitioners I spoke to shared my enthusiasm agreeing that there was a need for such a space. I sent for the details and began to research different ways of operating. Could we set up a co-operative on social enterprise lines?

To buy and renovate the building would be a huge financial undertaking in itself and then there would be the running costs to find. I would want to put in a full-time manager at the very least. Could it be self-sufficient?

Friends encouraged me with suggestions; I took photographs and began to create a 'treasure map' collage with a photo of the building in the centre. But I let the idea go. The property has been sold for conversion to a private residence. I hope its owners will love it and be happy.

It was a very large scale dream. Was my vision simply not large enough to take it on? Perhaps. I certainly didn't have the financial resources but I could have tackled that challenge had I felt ready to invest all my time and energy in making the dream a reality. I knew that I could paint the vision to enthuse others but as prime mover, I would have needed to commit years to chasing funds and managing the project. It just wasn't how I wanted to spend my time and I had to be honest about that.

"Is it your baby?", asked a wise friend. "You'll know in your gut if it is."

A business idea may be brilliant but it may not be brilliant *for you*. Sometimes we need to set the vision free to make its way in the world. It may be picked up by someone better placed to carry it through to completion. Who knows, it may be blown back to us on the wind some time in the future asking to be born.

DIAGNOSTIC PACK -
A SELF-COACHING SESSION

Ask yourself the following questions:

- Do you hate Monday mornings?
- Are you constantly distracted?
- Do you keep wishing you were somewhere else?
- Do you experience that sinking feeling when you contemplate staying in your present position?

If the answer is 'yes' to some or all of these, move on to the next stage.

Thinking of going self-employed?

- Have you taken a break long enough to be truly rested and refreshed?
- Have you confronted the negative features of your situation?
- Have you discussed it with trusted friends or associates?
- Do you feel a sense of relief at the thought of doing things differently?

Running a business?

- Have you had a holiday recently?
- Is this activity a drag on your business?
- Are there better ways of using your talents in the business? Easier ways to make money?
- Do you feel a sense of relief at the thought of doing things differently?

If the answer is still 'yes'...

Diagnosis: your horse is not in good shape

Treatment: if you can't fix it, dismount

Therapy: to inspire you and keep you motivated. See Chapter 8: 'Send For Fresh Horses'

Do you have an idea of what to do next? Write your ideas here...

How does your idea make you feel? Excited? Lighter? Terrified?

Have fun dreaming your dreams while you carry out your exit strategy.

Readers familiar with the concept will have spotted that 'emotional intelligence' is a thread running through what I'm saying. So, if you would like to know more about the idea read on. Otherwise you can skip to chapter 4!

EMOTIONAL INTELLIGENCE

Emotional Intelligence is now recognised as essential for effective living and working. The term, coined by researchers from Yale and the University of New Hampshire was popularised by Daniel Goleman in his now famous book 'Emotional Intelligence'.

Previously our Intelligence Quotient (IQ), which measured mental ability, was the predictor of success. But if we understand success in the widest terms (social, financial, relational) emotional intelligence (EQ) has been shown to be a more reliable indicator:

... "a study of children from a poor suburb of Boston suggests that 'emotional quotient' plays a significant role. The most powerful predictor of these children's success as adults was not their IQ – it was their ability, during their difficult childhoods, to govern their emotions, deal with their frustrations and cooperate with others."

What exactly is emotional intelligence? It involves being able to identify how we feel and how others may be feeling, to be able to understand the emotional landscape which is unfolding and therefore to be in a position to make choices about how we behave. Like any other truth about life, it is not new. Goleman prefaces his book with a quotation from Aristotle and the injunction 'Know Thyself' is attributed to Socrates.

Remember I said that your business is an extension of yourself? If you don't know yourself, you won't fully know and understand your business. Indeed it's possible to become so enmeshed in our business (or in our job) that we lose any sense of the point of it. "Why am I doing this? What is it all about?" Ignoring such promptings, we could be in danger of burnout and depression. Our judgement may be compromised and our working relationships may deteriorate.

Here is a quick guide to sharpening an important aspect of your Emotional Intelligence: being in charge of our feelings rather than at the mercy of them.

Do you ever get out of the wrong side of the bed?

Do you sometimes feel that nothing's going to go right today?

Would you like to be more in control of how you feel?

If you run your own business or work freelance, you'll know very well how much depends on you. If you learn how to recognise your emotional state, take responsibility for it and choose your attitude for the day, you can turn around a day which didn't seem promising at the start.

There are 4 steps to this which I have adapted from ideas I first encountered in 'Awareness' by Anthony de Mello:

Begin by connecting to how you are feeling right now. Sometimes, our surface mood disguises a deeper emotion. We may feel grumpy and out of sorts but if we take the time to sit quietly or reflect as we walk the dog, it may be that we discover we are still angry or disappointed about something that happened

39

yesterday. Identifying and naming the emotion is the first vital step.

Recognise that the emotion is in you. We sometimes attribute how we feel to the external circumstances be it the weather or someone that annoys us: "He *makes* me feel irritated/nervous/ inadequate." Separate out the circumstances from your reaction and you will find that you have a choice about how to respond. If you're not convinced, think of it this way. If you choose to be cheerful, the rain may still be falling and the client grumbling. The emotion is not in the rain or the client but in you.

You are more than your mood. Moods and feelings come and go but your core self remains. Try out the difference between saying "I am anxious" and "I have some anxious feelings". The first identifies the entire self with the anxiety; the second suggests that the anxiety, though present, is not the whole story. I find that this prevents me being overwhelmed by the feeling and affords a space to make a choice about how I will handle it, which takes us to step 4.

How do I want to feel today? It is important to acknowledge at this point that sad feelings may be entirely appropriate. Few of us get through life without experiencing loss or difficulty. In such cases, we may not be ready to 'cheer up' but we can still make a choice about how we wish to feel: calm? accepting? Maybe we need to express some angry or rebellious feelings before we can move into what the day brings.

Let's assume that no major crisis has arisen. You can get clear about the positive emotion you want to experience: motivated? light-hearted? optimistic? hopeful? Ask yourself what positive thoughts you can adopt and what actions you can take to promote your desired state.

Start the day by encountering yourself in these 4 steps:

Awareness, Ownership, Detachment and Choice. Your business will reflect the positive person you are choosing to be and when you meet other people, you'll be able to greet them authentically.

CHAPTER 4

GETTING OUT OF THE SADDLE

Getting out of the saddle is tricky if you've been in it for a long time. Muscles have stiffened, making dismounting a challenge particularly if it's a long way down or the ground is uneven. You need to pick the best spot if you don't want to land in mud or thorns and a helping hand doesn't go amiss. But you need to make a move or you'll be stuck there getting more and more saddle-sore by the minute.

In this section, we look at a range of business situations that require strategies for ending well. Before looking at these specific challenges, let's do some mental preparation.

Get your head round it

1. Plan For The Future

2. Reflect On The Past

3. Live In The Present

1. Plan For The Future

The future gets in the way of the present when our mind keeps straying to what we need to arrange, what obstacles we may encounter, how we are going to break news to people etc... I'm sure you can add to the list.

Forewarned is forearmed is a motto that suits me but it doesn't suit everyone. Like most mottoes and proverbs there is one to contradict it. *Don't cross your bridges before you come to them.* But it's not an *either/or*. The truth, as I see it, is not somewhere woolly in the middle but a genuine fusion of the two pieces of wisdom.

Survey the landscape as thoroughly as you can. Get a map and a timetable, read the guidebook, make your own list of things to pack and learn any new skills you're going to need. Set aside time for these tasks each day, week or whatever's appropriate. Do what you've chosen for that slot and then leave it alone and get on with the day.

A positive vision of the future is not only enjoyable, it's also essential for the realisation of your goal. But if you live *in* the vision to the exclusion of the here and now, you may miss good things around you and even worse, you'll be unable to enjoy the future when it comes because when it arrives it will be the present – which you've lost the art of living in!

So find a place to keep your plans such as a bag, drawer or a computer file. And when you put the stuff away, picture it in its place. When you notice you're thinking about it, picture the file and put the thoughts firmly inside.

2. Reflect On The Past

The past is an equally seductive place for our minds to dwell. The two contradictory sayings in this case can be combined as *Experience is a great teacher that nobody learns from*. We may not be very skilled at learning from mistakes but we're very good at dwelling on them, especially other people's! Unfinished business can clutter up our minds and entangle our emotions, preventing us from enjoying the moment and from moving on. Look at Chapter 5 if you want to cut straight to the de-clutter process.

But let's think about that quotation for a moment, because like most sayings, it contains some truth. At the global level, as a species, we seem quite incapable of grasping the futility of fighting. At the personal level, we regularly harm ourselves by abuse or neglect as though we had never heard of the dangers. We bury our dead horse and get a new one just like it.

Few of us are able to learn from the experience of others. It's how we're made: we learn best what we discover for ourselves – by doing or experiencing rather than simply by being told. I'll put on a jacket because I feel cold, not because somebody tells me to. This varies of course depending on how much of a rebel you may be!

But we often seem to be reluctant to learn even from our *own* experience. I would suggest several possible reasons for this:

- We have never formed the habit of reflecting on what we do, in spite of Socrates' dictum that the unexamined life is not worth living!
- If we look back, we may have to say, "I got it wrong"
- It hurts to remember disasters or losses.
- We plan to do things differently but fall into old patterns.

Let's look at these one by one.

Not reflecting

Some of you may have experienced personality typing or psychometric tests. Systems such as Myers-Briggs or the Enneagram tend to attract those already inclined to reflect on life and on themselves. The doers amongst us are more likely to regard this as a self-indulgent waste of time and 'just get on with it'.

Most systems will allow for the fact that though each of us may have a preferred way to function, there are benefits in being able to operate in modes not immediately 'natural' to us. To put it crudely, the doers can benefit by becoming a bit more reflective and those subject to analysis-paralysis can gain by just getting on with it!

We are inclined to ask "Why?" after a disappointment or disaster. This may yield useful information for future planning but it's important to be able to recognise when there are no more answers. Otherwise the 'why' question may hold us back: "I will not move on until I know", "I can't rebuild until I get the answer." And so on. The information may never be recoverable. It may never have existed in the first place. But we do have access to our own response – it may be all we have available to us. So that's what we have to work with. It's a bit like losing computer files in a crash. They're gone, so handle it.

"I got it wrong"

Have the courage to admit it, if only to yourself, and you'll find it's quite a relief. You can give up using all that mental energy demonstrating to yourself and others that it was somebody else's fault or that you had your finger on the pulse all along... How can we learn from experience, if we don't believe we have anything to learn?

Ever been called a control freak? The courage and vision and sometimes the sheer bloody-mindedness that you need to launch a business can have its downside. Fired with conviction, the entrepreneur is not always good at listening to others or at seeking and receiving support. "There are two ways of doing this – my way and the wrong way." Listening to others is the single most useful change you can make. You don't have to do what they suggest but you may learn something.

Do you do it 'my way' for fear of seeming vulnerable or incompetent? Let me tell you a secret. We're all making it up as we go along, or as a friend of mine once said, "It came as a great relief to me to discover that everybody was hand-knitting their lives just like I was." Soldiering on alone can be bad for your health.

Wilma says: *"my health was compromised through being 'burnt out'. In retrospect I should have allowed myself to accept more support and worked with others."*

"It hurts"

Yes, it does and dwelling on past misfortune saps our motivation. But the pain doesn't go away because we ignore it. It needs to be dealt with and as with our mistakes, there are lessons to be learned from it that we can take with us into the future.

Old patterns

Adopting new ways requires us to make a conscious and persistent effort to do things differently. We can make significant changes by becoming more aware of our own processes, by consciously choosing a new way forward and by adopting techniques to find and maintain a new course (see chapter 8).

3. Live in the present

The simplest things are the hardest to do it seems. Living in the present is one of them. A good example of living in the present would be the utter absorption of the dedicated gardener potting up seedlings. Oblivious of distractions and unaware of time passing, she may appear the perfect example. But the observer can't know whether her mind is focused on the seedlings or miles away planning a holiday or worrying about whether her daughter is eating properly.

To be completely in the present, her senses must be entirely engaged with the shapes, the smells, the touch of the plants and her intellect with the correct horticultural procedures. This is a state that very few of us reach. Buddhist monks practice for years to achieve 'mindfulness'. Our minds easily wander off and if we don't recall them to the task in hand, we are not in the here and now.

So now, let's get down to specifics...

LETTING GO OF THE DAY JOB

It's a big challenge to let go of the day job in order to start your business or become self-employed. You're going to need new skills and bring some unused ones back into play. You'll want to launch out in the right place at the right time and you need all the support you can get – of the right sort. Let's look at that first.

Family and friends will have plenty to say, not all of it helpful. Smile politely and ignore the doubters but pay attention if you think there's a grain of truth. Especially if it's an uncomfortable truth you're trying to avoid. I'll give you an example. A friend of mine said, "I hope you can stand the uncertainty. My brother-in-law spent the first ten years of his own business convinced that bankruptcy was just round the corner!" This was less than encouraging though I've had cause to remember the words on the occasions when there was more month than money! It was a sobering reminder that entrepreneurs need an ability to live with a certain level of risk. I'll have more to say about that later. As it happens, the company did very well and he and his family are now financially sound.

Another comment I regularly received was, "You're very brave!" Was that what they really meant? Maybe they were actually thinking, "You're off your head!" Was I?

Practical help is the best kind of support: whether it's introducing you to investors or stuffing envelopes. Don't be too proud to accept a helping hand. Accept any that's genuinely useful.

One of the lessons I learned was to listen to the plethora of business advice that's out there and then sift it carefully to pick out what was relevant for me. Business has fashions just like any other sphere and you will hear theories and slogans bandied around and all the more powerful because most of us want to sound as though we're up to speed. When you're new to the game, it's easy to be convinced that you must have a logo, or a USP (Unique Selling Point) or a website... Test the flavour of the month and decide whether it's the taste for you. Have the courage to reject what doesn't fit your way of working.

Because I had no business background when I set out 8 years ago, I took much of the received wisdom seriously even when, in my heart of hearts, I wasn't convinced. Tom Peters came to Glasgow some years back and told a large gathering of executives to tear up the 5-year plan! They were horrified – I was filled with glee. The point is not whether he was right or wrong; it is that (and I promise I will say this only once) it really is 'horses for courses'. It's got to fit you and your business if it is to work.

When you get out of the saddle, you need to find new allies. My best ones, not surprisingly, were people who were business owners and those, who like me, were starting out. The latter offered solidarity and a place to share triumphs and mistakes; the former gave me advice, introductions and sometimes referrals.

Network relentlessly. I'm lucky because it's like breathing to me. I can start a conversation in an empty room. You need to find your own way of doing it and there's lots of useful guidance.

Advice I found useful…

- You can't dine out on an expression of interest – wait till the cheque has cleared
- Exercise good credit control
- Being busy is not the same as being profitable

These nuggets of wisdom were useful to me because, as someone who has more ideas than I've got lives to put them into practice, it was helpful to have some advice that would help me keep my feet on the ground.

But if you're the sort that would naturally look after the detail then you're more likely to need encouragement to ask for the moon.

Advice I believed but didn't suit me...

Focus on a product, develop it, then market it systematically. This may work for you but it doesn't suit me.

I have given myself a hard time for engaging in too many different business activities and spreading myself too thinly instead of promoting a limited range of services. While sticking to a limited range of offerings may make sense, it just doesn't suit my personality. I thrive on variety and I have skills to offer in a wide range of related activities. As I said at the start, your business reflects who you are and if you force yourself into a mould that doesn't fit, you will not thrive.

When is enough enough?

Managing the transition into self-employment is often thought of as leaving security behind. Security, like nostalgia, is not what it used to be. Even the civil service, previously a byword for safe employment, is no longer the safe bet it once was. Restructuring, globalisation, changing demographics and the breathtaking speed of technological development is dramatically affecting even traditionally secure jobs. But it takes a while for popular 'wisdom' to catch up on reality. So going it alone is still regarded by many as the less secure option.

Certainly, we have to be prepared to create our own opportunities, we have to be open for business on the days when previously we dragged ourselves into work and hid behind a computer while we recovered from a hangover – or phoned in sick. Running your own business means that you'll have to be consistently proactive. That takes energy but it also generates it. Security is not a benefit if it saps your motivation and your creativity. And the freedom you gain from working for yourself allows you to take up opportunities that are closed to those who're working 9 to 5 for an employer.

The biggest challenge is deciding when to let go of the day job completely. I've known a number of would-be business owners who develop their idea or their service in their spare time, keeping on their job to pay the bills. This is fine so long as you are progressing towards the day when you will launch your business full time. Otherwise you have the worst of both worlds. You can't generate or accept enough work to make the business financially viable because you don't have the time. You can't throw yourself into your paid job because your mind is on the business. And as a result you can succeed in neither!

I was offered the opportunity of a contract that would give me my first 3 months of work. By good luck the company didn't want the work to start right away which gave me time to plan a start-up strategy and to leave my existing job.

What do you need to have in place?

Contracts? Financial cushion? A detailed plan? It's not the same for everyone.

Leanne needed: *"A way of meeting my basic living expenses and courage to leave my existing job, faith it would work out somehow and a strong network of supporters and encourager."*

Wilma: *"I started my first business as a training consultant in 1995. I had built up a prospect list through my business contacts and through doing freelance training in my spare time. So I started with a few contracts secured. I had worked out what I needed to earn to get by and had set targets for that (I achieved them and then exceeded them!)*

Leanne and Wilma talk about what they put in place before they made the leap. But sometimes we just have to jump. Nikki Wyatt did that 5 years ago when she realised she was caught in WUS, Waiting Until Syndrome.

The first major change in Nikki's life was precipitated by a sequence of events that began when she fell under a train in Milan Central station. You might think that was bad but things got even worse. This led her into therapy and personal development and after a period of reflection...

"I wrote down a vision of what I really wanted and acted on it. Within 24 hours, I was offered a job on a holistic magazine."

This move began a journey of learning and working in the area of healing and personal transformation but Nikki was still waiting for the perfect moment to become self employed. She was Waiting Until she...

"knew enough to be able to inspire others, had saved enough to make choices, had a partner who believed in me and a cast-iron business plan." When this insight dawned, she writes, *"I didn't wait for a train this time, I resigned from my job and left the station."*

Or to put it in our terms, she dismounted before the horse died and dropped her on the floor! But she trusted that her needs would be met in ways she couldn't yet see.

Her base of clients was building well so when she was offered a place on a Vibrational Medicine course, she accepted with no idea how she was going to pay for it. The school offered her a scholarship.

"once I got the hang of visioning and listening to the inner voice rather than the outer ones, life began to flow."

We are all at different points of the journey when it comes to trusting that our needs will be met. I must confess to having taken the "Pray to Allah but tie up your camel" approach, taking risks but knowing that I have some sort of fallback position. Sometimes my safety net has seemed very thin and very far away! Whatever level of risk you feel able to take will, in my experience, be rewarded.

THROWN OFF THE HORSE?

Carol was made redundant with very little warning and found herself with no job and only a modest package to keep her going while she decided what to do next. After spending a few days crying on the couch, she dried her eyes and decided to start up in business for herself.

"There was no doubt in my mind that I wanted my own business. From now on I would sink or swim by my own efforts." She set up a company to provide stress management services principally to call centres and developed it into an accredited training provider for vocational qualifications. But she admits to having, at first, only a vague idea of what she might do.

"My method was to edge along and test the water, then make a decision about which way to turn. Then I'd leave it to trust for a while and if it didn't work, try something else."

Nikki and Carol got out of the saddle in very different circumstances but both were clear that they wanted to work in a way which gave them more choice and more control over their working conditions. Both too, are willing to learn from experience rather than indulge in regrets. Carol had a good howl and started afresh. 7 years down the line, she adopts the same approach:

"...sometimes you realise that a certain project just hasn't worked. It's hard if you've put a lot of time and effort in to development, not to mention money. I have however found that any work or money spent is

never wasted, the experience itself is worth its weight in gold."

Wilma too has picked herself up after some painful changes. She wound up her business in Glasgow, sold her house and bought an apartment block in Oliva, Spain, with 3 flats, one to live in and two to rent out. The new business was a joint venture with a new life partner who subsequently took the decision to return to the UK.

"I sold my lovely house in Glasgow and gave up my business and financial success... My partner chose to return to UK 18 months later and that was a blow. However I continued alone and have no regrets."

CHAPTER 5

GRACEFUL DISMOUNTING FOR BUSINESS OWNERS

If you are already running a business, you will know that the big move from employment to self-employment is just the beginning! Change is still, paradoxically, a constant. It's likely that you'll experiment with different ways of doing things and it's important to know what to stick with and what to leave behind.

Most owners of small businesses are familiar with the distinction between working 'in' the business and working 'on' the business. Familiar it may be but it is, nonetheless, critical that you find a balance between the two. It is easy for the business owner to become immersed in the activities of the business, neglecting the planning, reviewing and envisioning that's essential for continuing success. When deliveries have to be met, invoices put out, and phone calls answered, it can seem less urgent to work out a marketing strategy, study the financial information, or read trade magazines.

Phil Olley suggests what he calls a 'hotel day' where he takes time out to work 'on' the business. It needn't cost even an overnight stay. There are plenty of hotels with large comfortable lounges where, for the price of coffee and a sandwich, one can sit all day with the laptop or just paper and pencil sorting out all the ideas that there isn't normally time for.

The rest of this chapter deals with closure ranging from specific communication skills all the way to the final challenge of handing over your business to the next generation.

ENDING A CONVERSATION

We've all met people who can't seem to get out of a room or off the phone. After you've both been through all the winding up and taking leave behaviour, they hover about saying "See you then" or "Thanks for calling." They may even restart the conversation. "That reminds me..."

Perhaps you've caught yourself in this sort of pattern. It's only a minor irritation in a social context but it can prove a handicap in other situations.

It is valuable to be able to bring an exchange to a close when you are:

- Selling
- Requests and proposals
- Advising, coaching and appraisal

Some of the reasons are common to all these situations. Your message will have greater impact if it is clear and uncluttered. A conversation that has continued beyond its natural life, is likely to be repetitive and rambling.

The maxim 'Quit while you're ahead' applies to them all.

Selling

It's possible to talk yourself out of a sale by missing the moment when the potential customer expresses a wish for the product. So anxious are you to convince, that you stop listening and continue talking beyond the point when you could have closed the deal.

I received a call from a pharmaceutical company asking me if I could work with three of their scientists. The brief was to run a series of report writing sessions to improve their skills in presenting findings for clients in a reader-friendly form. I sent along a few details about what I could offer and was duly invited in to meet their director. I was prepared with my sales presentation, track record and recommendations for a course.

After a few pleasantries, I heard, "Can we get some dates arranged?" I gulped, swallowed down my spiel and opened my diary. Once the dates were sorted, we agreed a price and I returned to the office to revamp my proposal as a confirmation document.

There is a good reason for having two ears and only one mouth. Forget sales TALK; adopt sales LISTENING.

Requests and proposals

If you are in the situation of presenting to a client or making a request to an associate or a potential funder, make the case clearly and concisely and then wait for the response. Don't attempt to fill the space with justifications and amplifications; this will only blur the original clarity.

If you are saying no to a request, do so courteously and clearly and then move on either physically or by changing the subject. If you hang around literally or metaphorically, the person may assume you want to be coaxed into saying yes!

Advising, coaching and appraisal

These roles involve a special sort of conversation where one party is leading or facilitating. It is his or her responsibility to guide the exchange to a fruitful conclusion in the time allotted. This is about the quality of the meeting as well as about its length. If you are aware of the clock, you are much more likely to use the available time productively – and you will end on schedule.

Unlike social conversation, exchanges with an agenda need to be structured in order to meet their aims. It's like the difference between making a movie and leaving a video camera running in the room. What you film may include interesting material but it will be shapeless and unsatisfying because it lacks the beginning, middle and end structure that moulds raw experience into a narrative. It's unsatisfying if a film or play ends in a sudden and arbitrary way for which we haven't been prepared. Simply to say "time's up" and round off a conversation as though it were a question in a pub quiz, won't do. Ending this type of conversation begins at the beginning!

Let's suppose an hour is the allotted time. First of all, agree or remind yourselves why you're meeting. Add to the agenda (formal or informal) anything that has arisen since a previous meeting. Often it will be appropriate to check out how the other person is or how events have developed since last you met.

This all sounds fine in theory but does it work in real life?

Beware the Narrative Trap

What I call the Narrative Trap can catch you when you invite the speaker to give you an update whereupon they launch into a blow-by-blow account of everything that's happened since you last met. Before you know it, twenty minutes of the allotted hour have already slipped past. Deal with this by supporting the speaker to summarise, to draw out insights and reflections from their narrative. Connect what they have said with the agreed agenda so that you can move the exchange from story mode into reflection or analysis and finally to action. This final stage may need about 25% of the available time depending on the nature of the conversation. It should include:

- Summarising the possible actions or decisions taken
- Selecting the ones that are actually to be put into practice before the next meeting
- Checking that the person is happy with this and has not been persuaded into agreeing

- Checking that everything important has been raised and that the person is not left without a resolution to an issue.

Naturally you can't expect to resolve everything there and then but it's important to acknowledge what needs attention and arrange for how it can be addressed.

ENDING A MEETING

The complaint about many meetings is that they make no difference. A good test of whether a meeting is worth the time spent is to ask what change has resulted. At the end of the meeting you should have moved on to a new place. If you're back where you started, you need to take a hard look at how you spend the time.

As with conversations, meetings are more likely to be productive and to end on time if they are well prepared. Formally constituted meetings have a set pattern to follow but informal meetings benefit too from a structured approach however simple. It can be a few headings on a piece of paper or written on a board so long as everyone present knows why they have met and what they intend to achieve in the agreed time. And do agree a time. Whether you're the official chair, the boss or the poor unfortunate in the hot seat, use that watch! I'm amazed at the number of people who try to run a meeting without keeping close track of time. Of course it runs away with them!

Allocate a time for each item to be discussed – you can be flexible with the time slots but they will help you steer through to the point where you need to begin rounding up.

Some regular forums are afflicted with long agendas of 23 items to be got through in an afternoon. This can arise when it's a challenge to get everyone together and there just is a lot of work to be done. Much though can be done in the preparation to check whether everything needs to be dealt with by *everybody* present. Can some of the items – e.g. those for information only – be dealt with by email? Can other issues be addressed by sub-groups? Rationalise the agenda as much as you can.

Any Other Business is a classic trap. If you include this at all (and you don't have to) make sure that items are agreed at the beginning of your discussions. Don't let it become a free-for-all lasting as long as the entire meeting. If an important issue arises that needs attention, agree a time limit for discussion after which you postpone discussion until the next available time.

You will find that, as people get used to this, at least some of them will use the time more effectively. A good chair will intervene to summarise when he or she spots the same points coming round again.

The usual ending to a meeting is the diary moment – a moment which can last a long time as you try to synchronise dates. Allow for it.

ENDING BUSINESS RELATIONSHIPS

Turning down business? Can I be serious? Very. Particularly when it's a lesson I'm still learning. When we've just started up, we accept every offer of work that comes our way don't we? For good reason. We need customers, we need income and we need experience so anything is worth a try.

But there comes a time in most businesses when choices have to be made about what to focus on and what to let go. A classic challenge for both business start-up and existing businesses is whether and when to let go of the 'bread-and-butter' jobs.

If we don't face up to it, we may fail to achieve our full potential because we're doing a lot of things quite well rather doing a few things brilliantly. It then becomes hard to let go of some of the work in order to attract more of the type we really want. We may fear:

- Losing income
- Letting down customers
- Becoming too specialised in a fast-changing marketplace

It's not just a matter of the number of hours in the day. The magic word is 'focus'. If our attention is diffused among a range of activities, the energy is limited for each. So how do we get out of that particular saddle?

- Ensure you've got enough business to allow you to take the risk of letting go in order to pick up more of what you really want to do
- Sub-contract or franchise the work so that you still get income from it
- Look after customers by passing them on to another provider
- Maintain enough diversity to allow for a flexible response to change

Just as a bar or even a shop has the right to refuse to serve a particular customer, you too can choose whether to continue supplying or working with a customer or client.

If they simply don't pay in time or at all, then the decision is relatively easy. It gets more complicated when it's a matter of their behaviour or their attitude. Do they 'mess you about' wasting your time and energy?

First it's important to remember that you are part of the transaction. Check whether you can improve the relationship by changing your approach

Early on in my business, I was delivering training to a client who, I reckoned, was not giving me the support I needed to give their delegates my best service. I would turn up to find the room locked and equipment missing. Sessions would be delayed or interrupted by administrative matters. What irritated me most was the fact that the person I dealt with was deeply defensive when I complained. This really lit my fuse and on one occasion (the only one) I actually lost it and shouted back at him.

A business-owner friend reminded me that he was representing the customer and it didn't matter how he behaved, I had to maintain my professionalism. *They* were paying *me* after all. Now that doesn't mean I should not ask for the level of support I wanted. But it made me aware that my reaction was about more than the practical side of things. He just got up my nose and I was allowing that to affect my responses.

The first step is to seek the client's co-operation. This is important because your reputation may be compromised if you have no control over the conditions in which you're expected to work.

Set up a meeting and explain how they can help you to provide them with the best value for their money. If they show no sign of being willing or able to change their approach, it may be time to end a relationship that isn't worth the revenue it's bringing in.

Debbie Jenkins in her Lean Marketing Champions ezine (www.leanmarketing.co.uk) writes:

So, How Did We Sack Our Clients?

We had a few to get rid of. One of them was our largest client for the previous 2 years, but when we investigated the economics of keeping that client we quickly realised that they were only just profitable for us. They were an 80 person consultancy. So our first strategy was to increase our prices by 100%. Now, remember we weren't trying to get a price increase, we were trying to find a way of extricating ourselves from the relationship.

They said they'd pay. Doh!

So, we held a very frank meeting with them where we discussed what would need to happen for us to work together in the future. I must say we were blunt. The main and recurring issue with this client was that they played "desperate" *all* the time. Every requirement was urgent, every piece of marketing material was needed yesterday. They never planned ahead and they were always ungrateful! So, we suggested ways that might work in the future. They promised to try!

Now, some people may be thinking, wow – that's so arrogant. And, you might be right. But, this is our business and if we're not enjoying it why are we doing it? We knew what we wanted out of our relationship with this client and we laid it on the table. They tried to change, but they were so ingrained in their old ways that it was impossible for them. So, we parted company!

We attempted a similar price rise with a few others we wanted to "sack" – with varying success. We tried a few other techniques, like recommending other companies who could satisfy them better than we could (we generated a few good partnerships with this model) and putting in longer timescales for projects.

But by far the most successful was being upfront and telling them why we were releasing them!

A Matter of Principle

Sometimes we discover that clients are involved in activities which don't chime with our values. This could be anything from connections with the arms trade to treating their employees badly. Very few of us have clean hands in the inter-connected world we live in and we have varying priorities. It's up to you to decide whose money you're comfortable taking.

"We're running a business, not a charity" is a familiar mantra dismissing any concern for factors outside the purely financial. This limited approach can be challenged not only on ethical grounds but also as an unsophisticated way of doing business.

Companies and government agencies are now beginning to look at more holistic approaches that take account of factors other than monetary ones: health and wellbeing, environmental impact, social responsibility etc.

There may be instances when you choose to continue a service out of loyalty or because you believe it to be valuable. Perhaps you provide a service which supports a non-profit organisation. Until you help them find an alternative, you may choose to continue even though it's not a major earner.

I stuck with a client for whom I delivered my least favourite service – it no longer gave me a buzz and I thought about finding someone else to provide the service. But they had been loyal customers who appreciated what I did so I decided to hang in. They subsequently landed a large contract, some of which was contracted out to my company. I was delighted not only to be offered the work but because this was an area which really did float my boat. I enjoyed every moment.

Sacking Suppliers

A similar strategy can be adopted with suppliers. If you are in a co-ordinating role, you have to be confident that your suppliers and sub-contractors will deliver to your standard. There's nothing more nerve-wracking than waiting for the brochures to arrive in time or hoping the wiring will be completed before the decorators arrive. Of course, if you're dealing with a trade which is effectively a seller's market, it may not be possible to take the work elsewhere. Your charm and negotiating skills will need to come into play. Get the best service by making sure that other businesses want to be associated with you!

Letting Go of Business Partners

Recognising when it's time to go your separate ways is not always easy. We may know that something isn't working but we're not sure what. We start to fall out over trivial things or we begin to avoid each other.

The process is fundamentally the same in all situations of ending:

- identify and name what's going on
- look for ways of sorting it

Friends of mine, Mary and Freda, wound up their business relationship amicably when they finally realised that they wanted different things from life. Mary had eyes on the big money and wanted to maintain a glossy lifestyle; after five years of successful trading in a small company, she also wanted the challenge of running a bigger organisation, of the type she had worked for in the past. Freda while eager for a certain level of prosperity, was motivated more by a wish for a balanced life. They began the process of separating out their financial interests, while continuing to trade to ensure that they gained the maximum from the business. After a slightly scary interim period, Freda landed a good job that gave her the security she wanted and the freedom to pursue other interests. Mary did indeed make some of the big money, as a director of two large businesses, but in the long run she settled for a more modest (and possibly more enjoyable) enterprise that she could integrate with her marriage and a lifestyle more appropriate to maturer years! They negotiated these changes with courage and, most importantly, without falling out. They are still good friends.

When you want your partner to go

Just like a marriage, there are things you only learn once you're actually working together.

Brenda says: *"I had the idea for a product that needed skills beyond my own so I approached someone I know well about progressing as a joint venture. Unfortunately I didn't read the real signals that he was not wholly committed. I wish I'd tested him more and earlier."*

John and Derek went in as equal partners to a business where, as it happened, John provided all the upfront capital. As time went on, it became clear to him that Derek simply wasn't pulling his weight; tasks weren't completed, phone calls weren't returned. John realised that he was carrying his partner. He resisted the temptation to have a showdown and took a softly-softly approach. He explained the difficulties as he saw them and asked his partner to say how it was for him. Rather than saying; "you haven't done what you said you would!" he asked open questions giving Derek the opportunity to explain what might be wrong. Derek offered little by way of explanation but not long after, he decided to pull out. John's non-confrontational approach had prompted him to 'consider his position'. What's more he did not claim anything from the business, a tacit acknowledgement that he had not contributed. This may seem too good to be true but it did happen and John would describe himself as something of a hothead. "I needed to learn another way of handling situations." Fortunately he learned in time.

What if your partner does not agree?

It's not working. You want rid of them to put it bluntly and they won't go... what then?

It depends on the status of your business relationship. One entrepreneur I met (we'll call her Mona) was, like John, generating most of the business and in addition discovering that her values didn't chime with those of her partner. But the partner wouldn't give up. Though not in a position to run the activities of the business, she was not prepared to pull out. Mona was forced to leave the name behind and continue her activities under a different one. There were legal procedures to go through but it was less expensive than taking the partner to court to force her out. It also allowed Mona to devote her energy to moving forward rather than wasting it on a drawn-out struggle.

In both of these cases, motivation plays an important part. If scoring a victory over the other party had been the principal motivation for John or Mona, they could have locked themselves into protracted legal wrangles and recrimination. To choose the best approach, you need to be clear about the outcome you want. If the answer is 'vengeance', then your ingenuity will no doubt come up with a plan. But beware the boomerang effect! If what you want is freedom to move on without the impediment of an unsuitable partner, then choose the route with the least risk financially and personally.

When your colleague leaves

The friend who has left the organisation has done so for something more suitable to him. He has not done it in order to leave you in the lurch though the effect may be that you have to continue a project without his input. You feel angry.

Step one is to identify your feelings. Perhaps you're avoiding him or not going to the pub on Fridays since you heard the news. If he comments, you say you've just been busy.

If you can acknowledge to yourself that you're angry, you've made an important start.

The next step is what to do about it. You don't want to blame him – after all he's doing what's best for him. Part of you is pleased for him. So look again at the feeling you called anger. Is it perhaps envy? Disappointment? Anxiety about completing the project without him?

Separating out what's going on allows you to make choices about your behaviour, if not your emotions. It makes it more possible to go for a drink and say something like, *"I've not had a chance to congratulate you properly, well done. If I'm honest, I was upset when I heard – I'll really miss your contribution."*

I'm willing to bet that your feelings will change as well as your behaviour.

This has the additional advantage of motivating you to address the practical problems. And it may mean that you get the best from him while he's there. The temptation could be to shut him out and lose what he can still contribute before he leaves.

Letting staff go

As ever, the end is determined by the beginning. Make sure you have all that you need in place with regards the terms of employment for your staff. Make sure, too, that you have access to expert support and advice on employment law.

I recently heard of a department in a large public sector organisation who set up a disciplinary hearing in contravention of the statutory requirements. Because the hearing panel included a representative of the management making the complaint, the hearing was invalid. The whole procedure had to be gone through again with the ensuing loss of time and revenue, not to mention the human cost in stress.

I confess to reaching the limits of empathy here. How do people get in such a mess when there are conditions laid down and bodies that can advise?

The lesson for the small business owner here is that we needn't feel at a disadvantage because of our size. Even big organisations need to take advice. Don't risk muddling along. If you do not have an HR expert to hand or a company to whom you outsource HR matters, your Local Enterprise Company (Business Gateway in Scotland) can help. Start with the DTI websites. www.dti.gov.uk/er/

Often we sense when employees lose motivation. They may be less punctual, take longer breaks, are off sick more often. Perhaps they avoid you, speaking only when necessary. It may be that they are preoccupied, worried about a relative. Maybe they've been dumped, maybe they've fallen in love and their head is in the clouds! Stay in touch with everyone so that you have an opportunity to gauge whether their preoccupation is temporary or a sign that they have itchy feet.

Beating people like slave masters to extract work from them succeeds only if there is an endless supply of labour waiting to step into the place of those who collapse. Anyone inclined to operate this way is unlikely to be reading this book. But it is easy to forget the irreducible truth that people work best for us when they are happy at work. Obsessed with the sales figures, excited by the new project, anxious about deadlines, months can go by before we lift our heads to look at our staff. When we do, they're looking the other way. Perhaps even at the job pages in the paper!

Some entrepreneurs are brilliant ideas people. Great at tackling tasks but not so hot on the people skills. Fired with enthusiasm, they can carry others with them or tread them under foot as they gallop past. If you recognise that you can sometimes be insensitive, you have two options. Develop your people skills or delegate that side of things to someone else. Ask your business partner or your manager to be your eyes and ears. Encourage them to learn and adopt a coaching style of management, which listens, not with a view to spying on staff, but in order to understand where they're coming from, to motivate them by showing that their contribution is valued.

I once worked for a boss who was regarded as somewhat cold and calculating. But his hard-headedness about his own career made him approachable by staff who wanted to leave. When asked for a reference, he was gracious and encouraging even when he genuinely didn't want to lose them. Honest enough to acknowledge that he too would go for the best offer, he recognised that his staff might do the same.

Open communication makes such a difference! It doesn't help the working atmosphere if staff feel they have to hide the jobs pages under the desk or stuff their tie back in their pocket when they return from a clandestine interview.

If they can be candid about their aspirations, they're likely to be more relaxed and more productive while they're with you. If you can redesign their job to meet their aspirations, they may choose to stay! Keep listening.

It may seem paradoxical but making the process of leaving comfortable and civilised does not, in itself, result in a rush to the exit. It is part of creating a safe and open working atmosphere where people feel trusted and so have no need to resort to covert behaviour or avoidance tactics. It could have a positive effect on staff turnover.

Succession Planning

There are many examples of the tragic waste of endeavour, which can occur because business owners fail to plan for their succession. Sometimes they just don't get around to it before it's too late. But it's more likely that they avoid thinking about it because:

- They don't want to face up to their own mortality.
- They have become so closely identified with the business that to lose control would be to lose a part of themselves.
- It may be hard to believe that anyone else could be trusted to run it.

The word 'tragic' is not, I believe, too strong a word because ironically the boss who won't face the issue may bring about the very oblivion he or she fears.

A family business with all the dynamics involved is particularly susceptible to the challenge of succession issues. When a senior family member is in the driving seat of a business, it is a bold son or daughter who suggests that they draw up a blueprint for the future. And yet a significant percentage of family businesses avoid succession planning whether they wish the business to be continued by family or non-family members.

An ostrich mentality cherishes the illusion that if we see or do nothing then nothing will happen. But we cannot freeze-dry the present circumstances; they will change in spite of us. So we might as well be in the driving seat rather than allowing our destiny to unravel.

Research conducted by the Caledonian Family Business Centre of Glasgow Caledonian University bears this out. Renee S. Reid, the centre director has this to say:

> *"Knowing that succession is inevitable, why do many owners not plan the process?"*

Most reasons contain an emotional element, such as letting go of something you have spent a life-time building; worries about the ability of your successors (who also happen to be family) or choosing between your children. This emotional element is extremely powerful and is often the reason why owners prefer to avoid planning all together.

If, as I've suggested, a business reflects the personality of its owner, a family business is bound to reflect the way that family functions. If communication is open and honest among family members, it is likely to be so when they are wearing their business hats. If the 'head of the family' makes all the decisions on the domestic front, it is unlikely that they will go in for power-sharing in the board room or behind the counter.

There *are* some good examples of succession planning, one of the best known in Scotland being Baxters of Speyside, now Baxters Food Group. The business is now headed by the fourth generation, who have returned from corporate careers to combine their knowledge and experience with the company's tradition of quality products. This is unusual. In spite of the fact that a large percentage of SMEs in the UK are family businesses, only a small proportion has survived into the second generation.

Gordon Baxter, the third generation boss, experimented with appointing non-executive directors to the board, an idea he imported from the US. This illustrates a willingness to take new ideas on board, which was undoubtedly one of the ingredients of their success.

According to the Baxters website,

In 1992, one year before the 125th anniversary of the founding of the business, Gordon handed over the Managing Directorship to his daughter, Audrey, and the fourth generation of Baxters took up the reins. Audrey had made a successful career for herself in the City with the merchant bankers Kleinwort Benson before succumbing eventually to the lure of the Highlands and the challenge of running the family business.

Now Chairman and Chief Executive, Audrey Baxter runs an organisation that has acquired companies in the UK and in Canada. Reading between the lines, it would seem that a rare combination of open-ness on the part of the older generation and commitment to core values on the part of the younger is at least a part of the secret which has seen Baxters expand from a small grocer's shop on Speyside to a global concern which remains a family business.

Such continuity could not have developed if the major players had hidden their heads in the sand and refused to contemplate a Happy Ending!

Get it in writing

It is easy to fall into the trap of thinking that there's no need for contractual agreements among friends. "Lawyers cost money and we trust each other, don't we?" As the owner of a small business, you may not have an HR manager to whom you can delegate; you are the one who has to handle potentially delicate matters with colleagues who may also be personal friends or family members.

Let's say you ask a friend to help out at a busy time. Presumably you agreed hours and payment when they started. Perhaps now though, they want fewer hours or a higher rate of pay. Perhaps you can no longer afford to keep them on. If there is no written agreement to provide an objective basis for discussion, it can be difficult to address, especially when friendship may also be at stake.

Many employment situations go wrong because expectations are not clear. A job description is a start but even that may not be enough. Your understanding of what's involved in a project may differ from that of your employee. Did you agree the timescale? Did they know exactly what their budget was? How far their decision-making authority went? Not only do these things need to be made explicit, they need to be regularly reviewed. Tasks and projects don't stay the same over time; they evolve and we discover requirements and consequences that weren't evident at the outset.

Recently I was asked to sign a confidentiality agreement with a company whose boss I know and respect. I had undergone an induction into their process, which included details about the product, which were the intellectual property of the company in question. The boss apologised for seeming heavy-handed but explained that they'd already had their fingers burned and had been advised to protect this new venture. I was happy to sign.

We wouldn't hesitate to put any other big project on a legal footing be it leasing premises, or securing investment funding. Neither should we hesitate to formalise other sorts of agreements.

The more we foresee and allow for at the beginning, the happier the ending will be!

InTENTions is a small company in Scotland which hires out colourful Indian wedding tents for celebration events. One of their business aims is to send a proportion of the income back to India to fund small businesses. This initially presented them with the particular challenge of being, as one of the directors puts it, "Tough and businesslike when dealing with nice-but-poor people" as well as "getting really stroppy with chancers trying to pull a fast one on us inexperienced beginners."

"The most important lesson we've learned is that it is absolutely necessary to get contracts and partnership agreements etc looked at by a lawyer to make sure there are no loopholes. Then, having learned by mistakes, forget them and move on positively. In our first year of trading we were too trusting and got stung, but by tightening up on contracts (such as payment in advance) we are a leaner, fitter organisation – though still a pleasant and helpful one to work with, we hope!"

CHANGING LOCATION

Giving Up Premises

A consultancy chose to raise their profile by renting premises, hiring reception and clerical staff and putting them in company livery. They had plenty of administrative tasks to delegate and they foresaw that they would use their premises for meetings with clients. It seemed a good decision but as time went on, it became clear that the overheads could not be justified. To put it another way, money was going into other people's pockets when it could be going into theirs.

To some extent it was a matter of timing. In the immediate post 80s climate, it was important for a growing company to look like one. But as technology made it increasingly possible to work effectively out of a home–based office, such an option ceased to be associated only with small fry. They also realised that effective consultants spend more time on-site with clients than they do in their own premises.

The company could have shirked the decision; it did after all mean letting staff go and could have been seen as failure. It also meant admitting that they had misread their market somewhat and got it wrong (never an easy thing to do) but they faced the situation and returned to working out of an office in the home of one of the partners.

Acquiring Premises

For Carol's company, the opposite decision was the right one. The time came to move out of the home office and rent premises. It had worked when there were only two full-time staff but as the business grew, more people came on board and although they met with clients on site, there were frequent visitors to the office from other agencies. So she took the plunge and rented a suite of rooms which provided a general office, a workspace and a small interview room. Within walking distance from home, it incurred no extra travelling cost and separated her personal and business life.

Differing needs at different points in the life of a business will generate different solutions. What will always be true is that you need a strategy for ending and moving on.

A physical move is a major disruption in the life of a business and all the chores and stresses we're familiar with in a domestic removal are compounded by the need to keep the business running at the same time.

If you have the personnel, appoint one person to manage the move and LET THEM GET ON WITH IT. If you're a one-person outfit, divide your time as far as possible between the twin demands – the move and the ongoing business.

Designate a space where the business can be conducted untouched by the surrounding upheaval, however tiny an island – a cupboard or a desk with a phone and a laptop. Guard it with your life.

Identify the absolute essentials for continuity once you've moved. Phones connected? Computers up and running? Refrigeration working? Packaging materials to hand? Make sure these are taken care of so that business can continue while the project manager continues to unpack and organise. As ever, I learned this from bitter experience.

Decanted

Five years ago, my house went on fire in the middle of the night, gutting the bathroom and upper hall and causing severe smoke damage to the upstairs rooms including the office. The cat and I escaped unharmed but I had to decant for 4 months while the restoration took place. The initial shock and chaos was considerable as you can imagine. Apart from my pyjamas, I had no clothes at all the morning after and only subsequently recovered some items, which though I was delighted to retrieve them, were unsuitable for the season or the task. Evening clothes and a winter coat in summer!

But importantly, I lost very little business information. The computer was cleaned up and the paper files were salvageable so I was able to set up a working space in the living room of the temporary flat to which I moved. It was at least 6 months before I raised my head above the parapet and saw how much the business had lost ground.

I had spent time negotiating with the loss adjuster and the insurance company, monitoring the builders' progress, arranging for furniture to be cleaned and restored, replacing carpets and choosing décor – the fun bit. It was endless. Had I been in a job, I would probably have taken some time off to sort things out and then struggled on as best I could. It would have taken even longer but at least I would have had money coming in. Working for myself, I had the time to attend to all these matters but it was time lost to the business and to my income. I didn't lose customers but I was working only part-time and I wasn't doing any marketing. The impact of that had its effect for some time afterwards.

The picture was clear to see when I looked back. But at the time I was probably in a state of shock for longer than I realised. My head was not quite together and my energy levels not yet back to normal.

What would have helped would have been to allocate a portion of each day to attend to the restoration process and then devote my attention to the business. Dramatic example though it is, it illustrates the need to attend to the important and not simply respond to the urgent. Draining the swamp while you're fighting the alligators.

MAKE IT EASY ON YOURSELF

Good habits take time to become embedded. Learning to do things differently is not a once-and-for-all event. It's a progressive development which takes place over time. I have sometimes felt disappointed and frustrated to find myself apparently back where I started as though I had slid back to the beginning in a game of snakes and ladders. This can happen in our personal or our business development. You'll remember it took Kate at least 5 resolutions to change before she actually did. But we need to be easy on ourselves. I'm sure that Kate got to know the landscape better each time she surveyed it. She wasn't starting from the same place.

If, in your business, it feels as though you're back at the starting gate, you won't be setting out again empty handed. You will still have your most precious asset, your knowledge and experience.

A friend of mine once likened it to looking out at the view from a round tower. As you climb the spiral staircase, you come back round to a window on the next level. The view is the same but your vantage point has changed. When it appears that we have returned to a habit or a way of thinking from which we thought we'd moved on, we're probably not in exactly the same place. We can view our situation from the perspective of what we've learned since we last found ourselves in a similar position.

The round tower is a useful image. It reminds us that *we* are the potential agents of change. The view from the tower is the same, it is we the viewers that make the difference.

'Up' is not necessarily better than 'down'. The higher you go the better the overview but from the windows near the bottom, you'll see more detail. Can't see the wood for the trees? Climb up a few levels. Full of great ideas but struggling to implement them? Climb down and take a closer look at the details.

CHAPTER 6

100 USES FOR A DEAD HORSE

The tender-hearted among you will remember with disgust a calendar of this nature featuring cats; those with a darker sense of humour laughed their socks off. I tend towards the latter in spite of being very fond of my own feline. You're running the Dead Horse Recycling Centre, how many ways can you think of to put the deceased beast to use? Here are some suggestions, add your own!

- Buried – as fertiliser
- Donated to science – for research
- As a guide to future design
- As a warning – what to avoid
- As an inspiration and model for new schemes

The point is obvious. Recycle. It's a waste not to. We've just been considering the importance of acknowledging the lessons we've learned. But that doesn't mean dwelling nostalgically on previous successes! Doing that, can trap us in the past and lock us out of the present.

So make some choices about what you want to keep and what you want to leave behind or throw out. Think of moving house. Some of us throw everything out and start again, some of us take the lot and cart an ever-growing pile of boxes from place to place. The rest of us will come somewhere between these two extremes.

Begin by picking out what will be really valuable for the future. Taking unwanted possessions to the charity shop is not the only way we can recycle. Skills, knowledge, confidence, and contacts can be used in different ways.

PACK YOUR SUITCASE

What will you put in it to take with you into the new life? Even when you're glad to leave the past behind, you will have learned some lessons. Put them in the case.

Difficult times may have shown you who your true **friends** are. Take them with you.

Maintain all useful **business contacts** by updating them with your plans – pack their details.

You have, as we saw in the opening chapter, successfully negotiated the obstacles you've encountered. Include your **survival skills.**

Talents and expertise from your previous life may come in handy in ways you can't predict. Don't lose them.

Fill your suitcase with your examples and anything else you can think of. Make it as specific as you can. Packing up your home and office may be a chore but it's a great way to learn about project planning and handling the unexpected!

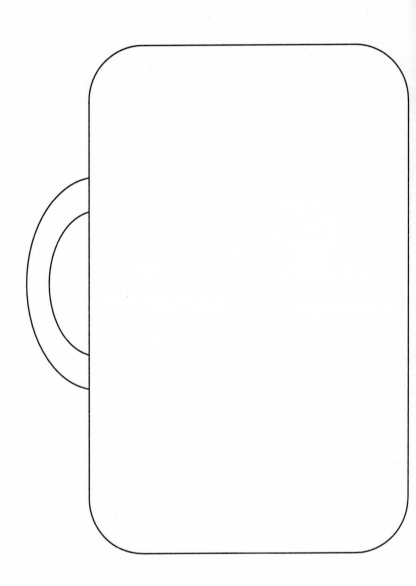

What's left in the pile can now be dumped. Resist the temptation to take the unsorted residue – literal or metaphorical – with you in bags and boxes. I plead guilty to this!

FILL THE BIN BAGS

Take your imaginary bin bags and start filling them. It's easy enough to throw out the *real* rubbish but it's harder to be ruthless when you come across something you were fond of or which seems to be valuable. But you need to get rid of the old in order to have room for the new. After all, if your arms are full of books, you can't pick up any more without dropping the lot!

That's why you began by filling the suitcase with what you actually need. Any item too good for the bin bag can be given away or sent to the charity shop. Unwanted gifts are often hard to part with. In your business life, these may come in the shape of advice which may be excellent in its own right but just not for you, like the stylish and expensive vase which looks awful with your living-room curtains.

ADVICE YOU DON'T NEED

If, like me, you are someone who readily takes advice on board then beware of the lure of the latest magic solution. Years ago when I first encountered personal growth and self awareness, I remember being warned not to replace one set of injunctions with another. In other words, you work to rid yourself of the voice that tells you you're no good. Instead of criticising yourself and others, you seek to be positive and affirming. But you try so hard that you find you're beating yourself up for not being positive.

I've had to watch out for this tendency in relation to my business. There always seems to be something that I ought to be doing or vital steps I need to take. So there's a constant nagging in my mind about say, marketing strategies or branding. One theory advocates systematic and detailed marketing techniques. Another recommends 'attraction' marketing which will allow clients simply to flow towards you effortlessly. And me, I swing between the two, resisting the discipline of the one and suspecting the other of being too good to be true.

Some business owners are allergic to advice, cynical about new developments and happy to point to bitter experience in support of their attitude. It's obvious that they're likely to miss the one really good idea that could make a difference. But a healthy scepticism is no bad thing. Because I didn't have a business background, I was perhaps too ready to give credence to what others said and lacked the confidence to trust my own reactions.

Take goals. What sort of goals work best? Smart? Stretch? Shabby? Sounds like a range of jeans! Or a pantomime:

"Goals should be realistic!"

"Oh no they shouldn't!"

"Oh yes, they should!"

SMART goals, should any of you actually have missed them, are:

- S = Specific
- M =Measurable
- A = Action Orientated
- R = Relevant
- T = Time Bound

Many have found this helpful but the panto hecklers say that goals should be out there in the stratosphere, otherwise we'll stay within our comfort zone. "Ask for the moon and you'll at least get the stars." Hence, 'stretch' goals.

Then along comes the iconoclast pointing out that we now have 2,500 permutations of what SMART stands for so even if they were once useful, they're now completely confusing. So what are SHABBY goals?

A fascinating online discussion ensued recently about the merits of this proposed new acronym:

- S = Subject
- H = Headline
- A = Actions
- BB = Business Benefits
- Y = Yes?

The contributor John Driscoll was forced to confess that he hadn't been entirely serious, after he received a flood of responses to his article. SMART supporters rose to its defence, others swore immediate allegiance to the new 'dress-down' goal concept. One contributor reminded us of yet more acronyms including POWER

- P = Positive – Is the objective/outcome stated in the positive?
- O = Ownership – Who is involved? What will you be doing?
- W = Where, When, What, Who – get the specific details for each area
- E = Ecology – What problems could achieving this cause for you/others?
- R = Real – What would you see/hear/feel/sense if you had achieved this?

And the moral of this story?

DOES A TOOL WORK FOR YOU?

Is it appropriate to the task and the context? For example, Bill Reed says, *"Show an East Asian manager a target that fits the 'achievable' box and he (sic) will express his disappointment at the lack of ambition and drive."*

Don't spend so much time arguing about the tools when you could be simply getting on with the job.

Whatever theory you opt for, make sure your actual goals are yours alone:

- Treble your turnover in a year?
- Revolutionise Scotland's health through raspberry production?
- Teach the world to sing?

A borrowed goal is no use to you. This is the only occasion when an own goal is a good thing!

Let's be fair. Ideas evolve and a good idea is often replaced with a better one. But there are a number of lessons here to be learned if you are to avoid becoming a business health fad junky.

Listen to your first response to an idea or a piece of advice. It may not be your final settled opinion but note it. Test your reaction against the views of others. Let me share my close encounters with the USP.

When the concept of a Unique Selling Point (USP) was explained to me, it seemed like a tall order. I envied those who seemed to have thought of a product that was completely new; or those who'd hit upon an original version or a fresh angle on an old favourite.

The service I had to offer was sound and I was good at what I did. But original it wasn't and certainly not unique. Perhaps if I'd asked around, I might have discovered that I wasn't the only one failing to identify the unique features of a perfectly ordinary but useful product.

Then to my delight, I read Debbie Jenkins' Lean Marketing Champions (www.leanmarketing.co.uk) article *Why USPs Don't Work*. It was the first time I'd heard anyone challenge the concept – apart from my own wee inner voice. Even more important for me than abandoning the USP search was the discovery that I could learn to trust my own hunches.

Sieve out the dross and keep the nugget of useful advice. There *is* a value to thinking in terms of USP. It forces you to think hard about exactly what you're offering, to look at your competitors and to examine the effectiveness of the image you project. But if you use up precious working hours looking for the Holy Grail of a description that nobody else in the entire universe is ever likely to think of... well, I rest my case.

Whether it's a USP, a goal, or a business plan, be prepared to throw it out and get a new one. Remember Tom Peters tearing up the 5 year plan!

Earlier I talked about the wisdom of working 'on' the business as well as 'in' it. If you seize on every new idea you encounter, pursuing it with a convert's zeal, you could be in danger of reversing the process in a way that isn't helpful. You risk spending so much time 'on' the business that analysis paralysis sets in. Sometimes we just need to get down to it and do the work.

Okay, you've thrown out or recycled what you don't need and you've packed your case with what you do need for the future. It's time to say goodbye.

CHAPTER 7

GIVE THE HORSE A GOOD SEND–OFF!

THE IMPORTANCE OF CLOSURE

Whether an ending has been forced on us or is a choice, it's important to round off well. Even if you're glad to see the back of places or people, it's good to acknowledge what we're leaving behind before we move on. To achieve what we've come to call 'closure', we need to follow through on our confidence that we're doing the right thing and broadcast our intentions. No folding up our tents and slipping off into the night! Apart from being ungracious, it doesn't do much for your credibility. Be upfront. Throw a party.

Deaths and funerals are classic opportunities for acting out stored up grievances. How many family feuds have come to light or had their origin at the wake? Don't let your farewell party turn into a brawl. Get the skeletons out, brush them off and bury the bones beforehand. Otherwise they may fall out on to your head when next you open the cupboard.

Whether you're leaving your job to start a business, or winding up a project, a leave-taking celebration has lots of benefits. Shortly before she set off for Spain, Wilma hired a venue and issued an open invitation to friends and business associates to drop in and say 'goodbye'. By that time, she was worn out by the physical and mental management of the move not to mention the vagaries of the euro prevailing at the time! The farewell event not only allowed her to see everyone but gave her exhausted spirits a huge lift. Around 80 folk turned up to cheer her on her way, and she set off on a wave of good wishes and encouragement.

Such an event does more than simply say farewell. We learn more about why people value us and we may be surprised by the sheer amount of goodwill we have gathered. And, of course, it provides an opportunity to talk about the new project. Wilma was ready with contact details and special opening offers for her holiday flats. Very much a case of 'on with the new'!

And as we've seen , a major change presents us with decisions about what to take and what to leave behind. The farewell bash could include a bonfire of all the old papers you've been meaning to clear out! And anyhow, do you really need an excuse to party?

You will need to conclude your affairs well if you are to move forward gracefully. Some people have no option but to 'clear their desk' and leave the building. If you're leaving a job, I hope you will be allowed a more dignified exit.

It may seem to be stating the obvious to say that it's a good idea to round off tasks, tidy desks and filing cabinets but the reality is often otherwise. You may have suffered from a predecessor who gave up and stuffed unfinished work into a bottom drawer. Perhaps the person handing over to you was 'economical with the truth'.

You, of course, would not stoop so low. However tempted you are to take revenge by laying a few booby traps for your successor, resist. Even if they don't rebound on you, the satisfaction will be short-lived.

"Hoist with his own petard" is Shakespeare's way of saying "What goes around, comes around." And I don't believe his words were merely pragmatic. There's a higher order of self-interest involved. Spite contaminates the perpetrator as well as the victim. If you want a happy ending, make sure you leave cleanly.

If it's a business you're closing, then make sure you let everyone know that you're about to cease trading: suppliers, customers, and contacts. Even if you think you'll never see them again, you never know when they might reappear. You want to be sure you keep them onside. The more open you are, the less anyone is likely to think that you're up to anything dodgy.

Your accountant and your legal adviser will keep you right on the technical side of winding up. There are some agencies listed for you to contact if you need help with this.

But, I hear you say: "I dread a leaving do. I hate goodbyes." Okay. Maybe a party isn't for you; it's not your style to wave a white hanky from the cliff top until the ship is out of sight. The danger is that in your dislike of parting scenes, you may overlook some of the essential rounding–off processes. Do your own thing but do *something*. Just don't go into denial about it.

LEAVING TO START YOUR BUSINESS?

Some new businesses have a clear start date and open with a fanfare. Others evolve in a more gradual way. Lots of people keep on the day job while they experiment with the business in their spare time. They go part-time thus easing the transition towards full self-employment. Depending on your temperament and the nature of your business, this can work well. But as I've mentioned, there are drawbacks in trying to swim with one foot still on the bottom. An opening launch is a great way to mark when the old life ends and the new one actually begins.

We need to make a statement about who we are now, not only to the watching world, but also to ourselves. Particularly if you do not have a business background, there is a significant shift to make in your identity from employee to entrepreneur. One of my business contacts tells me that setting up her business had felt like building, decorating and furnishing a house without actually moving in. She visited it but only after 18 months did she feel that she 'inhabited' her own business.

If, like John, you give up being a financial adviser to run a cheese shop, people can hardly fail to notice. But if you continue in the same trade, be it journalism, IT or hairdressing, the only difference to the outside world is that you're in business for yourself.

Having a party or sending out your announcements means you can't hide any longer. You're putting yourself confidently out there in the marketplace. Scary? I was interested to see that a Business Gateway website recommends the Susan Jeffers classic 'Feel the Fear and do it Anyway', an acknowledgement that business information is not enough. How we feel affects how we do business – or even whether we make the leap and do it at all.

Adopting the driving test tactic (tell nobody you're sitting it then you don't need to tell anyone if you fail) will not work. You can't run a successful business on the quiet!

Yes, you will market test your product or service but sooner or later, you have to go for broke.

CHANGES IN YOUR BUSINESS

Earlier on, we considered some of the endings we may have to manage: ceasing a business activity, discontinuing a product, ending a contract or a business relationship, moving premises etc. Is it helpful to celebrate all or any of these?

Whether or not partying is appropriate, it is certainly important to have a clear end point. A physical removal leaves us no option; we simply have to shift our stuff by a certain date.

Once when moving house, I forget to check a couple of cupboards and received a phone call from the new owner to say that my pots, pans and casserole dishes were in the front garden and would be taken by the council if I didn't come to collect them!

But other sorts of change may not offer such an unavoidable deadline, so being clear about when the change takes place will remind us to update web pages, change answerphone messages and generally tie up loose ends.

The construction industry has traditional rituals marking the stages of a building project, laying foundation stones, topping out and so on. Sometimes a date for this has to be fixed well in advance to accommodate diaries. Having put down these markers in the timeline encourages effort towards meeting them even if progress does not go entirely to plan. Such is the complexity of the operation one could imagine the drift that might easily set in if no such events were scheduled.

What if your ending is an unhappy one: a business relationship that didn't work or indeed the winding up of an enterprise that didn't succeed as you'd hoped? It is tempting to keep our mouth shut and hope nobody notices. But usually there are practical reasons for letting it be known. You can avoid offence or muddle by letting the relevant people know about the impending change.

Only this year, I advertised an event for which not a single person signed up. Because of commitments to venue and caterers, I had to agree a clear cut-off date for cancellation in order not to be liable for costs. So in spite of my chagrin I had a strong financial incentive to let everyone know in time! Being relatively new to the area, I was keen to establish a reputation and was not looking forward to making the cancellation calls.

But all the suppliers took it in their stride. Some were sympathetic and supportive; everyone appreciated that the deadline was honoured without losses incurred. Nobody was shirty or critical. After all, they're in business too and know about the challenges and the need to experiment with what works and what doesn't.

As it happens, I discovered not long after, that a more experienced competitor had also been forced to cancel an event for lack of bookings. I was reminded yet again that I have a tendency to assume that others have got everything sewn up and sorted. The reality is that they too sometimes fall off their horses and have to dust themselves off and remount!

I have re-advertised the service in a different format and await results. If this horse proves not to be a runner, what then? Could I 'celebrate' a non-event? Well my first thought is that the very announcement that it will no longer be on offer might stimulate demand from the undecided. And who knows how it could then develop?

If it really has to be declared dead, then I would announce what elements of the service I will continue to provide and in what form. And I would cryogenically preserve this horse until the world is ready for it!

And what if you haven't foreseen the end in time to put your horse out to pasture? It drops under you and you face the receivers or the bailiffs? Hardly party time is it? More like a wake! And that's not such a daft idea. Only the dishonest need to hide in shame. There may not be cash to spare for the bubbly but you can still mark the horse's passing. A wake often includes reminiscing about the deceased, sharing memories good and bad and making discoveries about things we never knew.

You can gather together everyone who has been involved in the enterprise and do just that. You can note your successes and the lessons learned; you can thank everyone for their involvement. Not all of the information will be music to our ears but it's all part of making sense of what has happened and of our own part in it. If you can't get together physically, email round or send out cards.

Managed endings are happier endings. Is that any more than a trick of language?

I guess what I'm saying is that endings are easier to deal with if they are seen as part of an ongoing process. The seed in the ground, the fallen and rotting tree that becomes a host to smaller life forms. The paradox here is that we deal with that more easily by celebrating changes rather than ignoring them.

CHAPTER 8

SEND FOR FRESH HORSES!

LESSONS I'VE LEARNED

The horse is honourably buried, we've tidied up after the party and now it's time to move on. In this final chapter, I'll bring you up to date with my story at the time of writing. I'll then go on to share with you the tools which I've found most powerful in working with clients who wanted to make significant changes themselves.

If a happy ending is indeed to be a new beginning, we need some idea of what we're going to do next. Those who've been thrown off suddenly may have to start from scratch. Those of you who knew it was time for a change may already have some ideas in mind.

Chris says: *"We never stay on a horse that long. As soon as we feel our mount or ourselves tiring, we look around for a fresh challenge. There are always so many possibilities!"*

How do you assess those possibilities? There is a lot said and written about creating a vision for your business – and plenty about goal-setting and targets. I don't intend here to repeat what you can read elsewhere. In the suggested reading list, you'll find my favourites. Among them is Stephen Covey's classic 'The 7 Habits of Highly Effective People'.

In it, he makes the point that before a project takes physical shape, it takes shape in our minds. If it is fully thought out, it is more likely to shape up well and without the waste that results from setting a mistake in concrete. But he goes on to say that even if we don't consciously plan, there will be a design in our heads, a default design which we've learned or picked up without noticing.

When I look back on my earlier life, it feels as though I was on a conveyor belt. Liz Lochhead expresses this in these lines from her poem, *The Choosing:*

I think of the prizes that were ours for the taking
and wonder when the choices got made
we don't remember making.

These days I live and work more consciously. Creating a design allows me to be in the driving seat and not borne along by default. The route may take some surprising turns but the general direction is intentional.

In the autumn of 2003, I put my small terrace house in Glasgow up for sale. After the fire, I had taken a few trips down to the coast to look at property but once I moved back to my restored home, I settled down for another 3½ years. Now I was hankering to be out of the city and preferably by the sea.

Some friends were surprised that I was willing to sell the house before finding somewhere else. But it made sense to me as a self-employed person, to know what I would have to spend. I looked in coastal areas near enough to Scotland's central belt to make it practical to continue my work with clients. But nothing felt quite right. So I did what I do with coaching clients. I took a blank piece of paper and asked myself what 10 out of 10 looked like as regards location. I wrote 'Bute' in the middle of the page. For those of you unfamiliar with the West of Scotland, the Isle of Bute is in the estuary of the river Clyde between Arran and the mainland coast. The journey to Glasgow for example, takes about an hour and a half. I love water and boats so the prospect of having to board the ferry for the half hour journey to the mainland was a positive delight – and still is.

This revelation did not come entirely out of the blue. A couple of years previously I had spent a weekend there in fabulous weather (Bute has been called Scotland's Madeira) walking with a friend. As you do, we talked about the place which once had been a holiday resort for Glasgow workers who flocked in their thousands to Rothesay for their annual 'Fair' holiday. The island boasted the UK's only offshore tramway which took holidaymakers 6 miles from the pier to a beach on the other side of the island. Like many such resorts in the UK, it declined with the rise of the foreign package holiday trade.

Its former glory could be seen in the Victorian architecture of the town and the rest of the island had a kind of peace, which soothed the spirit and restored a sense of perspective to the city-jaded mind. What role could it now play? To me it seemed like a place of wholeness and healing.

I had forgotten all this theorising, or so I believed, until the word Bute appeared on my page. At once, it became not only a possible place to live but also the opportunity for a new business venture, running holistic breaks with a coaching emphasis. That evening I was due to meet a friend for a meal and was soon telling her about the bees that were buzzing in my head. I hadn't known that she had spent the first 6 years of her life on the island, both sets of grandparents owning pubs! The following day I had a lunch date with a business friend who took up the idea with excitement. She reminded me of a mutual friend who had useful business connections with Bute. All this within 24 hours!

As soon as I had a day free, I was off down to Bute to investigate. By this time, I had sold the house and committed myself to a pre-Christmas entry date. Houses on Bute tend to be large – the aforesaid Victorian piles – or small flats dating from the holiday letting heyday. Many needed a huge amount of renovation for which I didn't have the time nor energy. I settled for a 6-month lease on a small rented flat in the fishing port outside the main town. It had a view down a side street to the waterfront. The January day when I arrived to pick up the keys was clear and sunny. The air smelled of seaweed evoking memories of childhood holidays. I knew I had done the right thing.

No matter what lay ahead I was in the right place and that had to be the foundation for whatever came next.

So what lessons did I learn?

I stuck to what I knew was essential for my well-being and held to what was true for me:

For example, one reaction I got was "January!? What on earth are you doing moving down there in the middle of winter?" But the worst weather we've had since I came here was in the August of 2004 when monsoon rain caused landslides not just here but across the UK. As it happens I was blessed with 6 weeks of extraordinarily sunny weather in February and March and I have the photos to prove it. But even without this stroke of luck, I was quite willing to accept and enjoy what the weather served up. The countryside has a different beauty in winter and I wasn't, after all, going for a beach holiday; I was going to live and work all the year round.

Renting the flat understandably evoked the positive response, "Very sensible. That will let you try out living there before you commit yourself." I would nod agreement knowing all the while that I was here to stay. Don't ask me why I was so certain. I just knew that I had no intention of returning unless some external circumstance made that necessary.

I kept the desired outcome in view and worked out the practicalities that ensued from that instead of allowing the practical problems to dictate the decision.

For example, how was I going to earn my living? I hoped to develop the holistic breaks idea, my coaching was often conducted by phone and I intended to travel to existing customers even if this meant spending part of the week in the city. That was my safety net. In practice my working life has unfolded rather differently – more of that anon or elsewhere. I guess I can go ahead without seeing the whole of the map so long as I can shine enough light on the section in front of me!

I accepted help

I had no shortage of accommodation offers from friends for a bed for the night or temporary office space.

A VISION FOR THE FUTURE

Did you have a clear vision of the future? I asked my business-owner contributors. We've already seen that for some the vision suddenly unfolded while for others it unrolled as they travelled along. I recognise both of these processes. The vision of going to Bute appeared unexpectedly but there were components of the vision about which I was absolutely clear. So for me, it felt less sudden than it appeared to others.

Now that I'm here, my working life has taken some unexpected turns. By the time you read this, the picture may be different again! But I distinguish between the product and the process. I may stop providing some services and start providing others. I may spend more time writing and less time speaking or vice versa. But I know what my working life needs to contain for me to be happy and effective.

ASK YOURSELF: WHO DO I WANT TO BE? HOW DO I WANT TO FEEL?

These are not the first questions we're accustomed to address in the traditional business plan, but without them our market surveys and financial projections will not be soundly based. Lest such questions seem to you relevant only to the 'softer' professions, let me tell you the first ones I was asked by a hard-headed business adviser whom I consulted about the Bute Holistic Breaks idea. They were, in this order:

- How old are you?
- How hard do you want to work?

That gave me something to think about! In the introduction I said that our businesses cannot but reflect who we are. My adviser understood this in a very practical way in terms of the physical and mental resources I was able and willing to commit. I'll add a third question to his:

- Exactly how do you want to spend your time?

I ask this because some people start a business based on their passion for say, woodturning or games design, and find that only a percentage of their time is spent on the occupation they love. Make sure that you'll be able to spend your time doing what you're best at;

outsource or employ others to do the tasks you prefer not to do.

If you anticipate being a sole trader, list the tasks essential to the business and draw a pie chart to see how much of your working week will be spent doing what you want to do – and whether you will also have time to eat and sleep!

WHO DO YOU WANT TO BE?

It's been the practice to hold up the big name entrepreneurs as role models for the rest of us. If you're inspired by them, that's great. But not all of us want to be a millionaire or see our names blazoned across the sky. Plenty of people aspire to the independence of creating a comfortable lifestyle with some time for themselves and their family – to be traders rather than tycoons. Decide what *you* want.

For Leanne it was personal fulfilment:

I wanted to do a job that inspired me, kept me true to myself and constantly reminded me why I was here.

For Wilma: *"The motivation for my first business venture was to provide the type of training that I wanted to, rather than be training within the company who gave lip service to it."*

However there was another new beginning in store.

'I gave this business up 8 years later because I was discontented with my life in Scotland (work and weather!) and wanted to do something completely

different. I fell in love with Spain and decided to move there, as it was something I'd longed to do. It was a 'now or never' move'.

For both Wilma and Leanne, their choice of occupation was part of a wider choice involving their values and the totality of how they wanted to spend their lives.

Some people love the buzz of creating a business for its own sake – it doesn't matter to them if they make widgets or windmills. When it's flourishing, they diversify, sell it or create a franchise, leaving them with the wherewithal to move on and begin a new enterprise. Others are more interested in the activity itself. If you love cooking, you don't want to sit in an office managing a chain of restaurants. You want to be in your kitchen creating wonderful food.

And what about making money? Isn't that what's it all about? Again you have to be clear what priority it has for you. Profitability is a measure of success and an essential for survival. But if you were to offer the classic entrepreneur the choice between staying in the same line of business or risking making less money by starting a new venture, she would be more likely to choose the latter. The excitement is as important as the money and sometimes more so.

BE IT NOW

While you're contemplating dismounting, while you're waiting for the next horse to be shod, while you're riding to the next staging post, you can still be who you're meant to be, giving and receiving, wherever you are and whomever you're with.

I've always loved a saying by Annie Dillard, "The way we live our days is the way we live our lives." In other words, it is *how* we do what we do that matters.

Even an apparently ordinary day can be infused with the qualities we would wish to bring to our most cherished project. "What do you want to be when you grow up?" children used to be asked. Perhaps the question should be *"How* do you want to be?"

Don't let the quest for fresh horses be the end in itself. I read once that self-improvement is a typical preoccupation of mid-life prompted by an awareness of the passing years. It's no bad thing to seek to make the most of the time given to us. But two things occur to me:

First, time is not about hours and days measured by the clock. When we are young, it feels as though there is all the time in the world. Most of us as we get older have the experience of time passing more quickly and of wondering who stole the last 5 years while our backs were turned! I can think of periods in my life that seem infinitely more significant than the actual time span they occupied. So, yes, let's use the time available without fretting about whether there's enough of it.

Second, self-improvement as another proficiency badge to sew on our sleeves is a limited activity with the focus on the 'self' part. It is what has been called an 'ego project'. It is one of life's many paradoxes that in order to be truly ourselves, we need to leave our self behind or at least the layers of self that cover who we truly are, sloughing them off like a snake to reveal the new skin beneath. And why would we do that? Particularly when it's painful?

To answer that I quote Chris again. *"It can seem like the end of the world sometimes, when a heartfelt project fails. But in the longer term one can see the benefits of change - even painful change. Everyone can be a winner, even in the face of disaster. Coping with adversity usually results in spectacular personal growth."*

That flexibility and optimistic spirit seems to be a characteristic of the entrepreneurs I know!

Julie: *"If it doesn't pay off, we'll do something else instead."*

Wilma: *"I believe there are always options, and no matter the path we choose, there will be other options later on."*

Carol: *"If it doesn't work, try something else."*

There was a time when I had difficulty reconciling this willingness to adapt and move on, with the emphasis I kept encountering on being 110% committed to a goal. How can we have our eyes fixed on the goal and be scanning the horizon for other possibilities?

The principle of non-attachment may be familiar to some of you: this means committing oneself to a course of action, a goal or a wish and then detaching from it in the sense of breaking the umbilical cord that binds us to it. It is still ours but our identity is not bound up in it. We will take it or leave it, not because we are indifferent but because we trust that the best outcome will transpire. I'm reminded of the old Scottish saying: "Whit's fur you, will no' go by you." For many years I thought of this as a piece of superstition of the, "If the bullet's got your number on it...' variety. But now I see it in a different light.

I will not miss what is 'intended' for me because I have fine-tuned my vision to mesh with the possibilities that are available to me. I will also select and be drawn to some people and events in my environment and not others because that's what I've set my radar to detect.

People explain this in various ways citing everything from quantum physics to the action of the angels. I'm ignorant of one and agnostic about the other! I find it easier to think of the image of a spider's web where the tiniest vibration of an insect sends a tremor through the whole system.

So what does all this mean for vision creation and goal setting?

We need to commit to a course if we are not to be blown around in the wind. But we need to check our position and correct it if necessary – that's where the flexibility comes in. We may need to be willing to change course completely but if we are clear about the destination, we will get there by a different route.

The realisation of the vision may be in a different form from the one we first described to ourselves.

Leanne: *"I wanted to do a job that inspired me and kept me true to myself and constantly reminded me why I was her."*

She will succeed if she keeps the vision polished, although it may take a different shape from the one she first envisaged.

For those with a huge commitment to a very specific goal – to be the largest organic market garden in the UK, let's say – a more single-minded approach will make sense:

"Whatever your ultimate destination, whatever your dream, think about it all day long, every day, until one day you wake up to discover you've arrived."

To some extent, it's a personality thing. Some of us are dedicated, single-minded – did I say 'obsessed'? – individuals who simply refuse to contemplate any other outcome. Others taste and try a variety of options from life's bazaar. But contrary to the song from 'Joseph and his Amazing Technicolor Dreamcoat', *any* dream will *not* do.

SHAPE YOUR DREAM WITH THE 'VISION TOOL BAG'

Your bag contains the following items:

- The 'How Do You Want To Feel?' Gauge
- The Vision Thing
- Be-Do-Have
- Letter From The Future
- An Anti-Saboteur Device

The 'How Do You Want To Feel?' Gauge

How do you want to feel? Motivated, liberated, healthy, wealthy, excited, safe?

Write *your* answers in the clouds. Unearth your feelings and let them float.

The Vision Thing

What does 10/10 look like, sound like, feel like? Put your response (a word, a phrase or an image) in the middle of a large sheet of paper. Then radiate out from the centre, filling in all that you need to have in place to make that vision possible. Whether you use words or pictures (cut out images from magazines if graphic art is not your thing), be sure to create a colourful collage. Hang it on the office wall to inspire you!

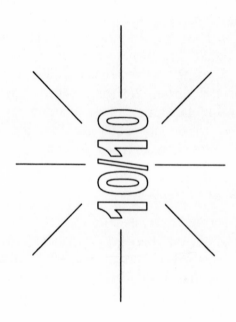

Be-Do-Have

The Be – Do – Have approach reverses the way we often think:

*I need to **have** premises in order to **sell** my work in order to **be** a silversmith.*

Turn it around:

Be a silversmith, **sell** your work and then you can **have** premises.

Think about it, having a state-of-the-art workroom and shop is never going to turn you into a silversmith. Okay you may say, *I can see that, but how can I run my own business, without any resources?* I'm not suggesting you can. What I'm saying is that we often stop ourselves because we're thinking about the cart instead of the horse. We get bogged down in the practical obstacles rather than focusing on how we want things to be and then tackling the practical challenges that will make it so.

*I need to **have** money in order to **start up** my business then I'll **be** an entrepreneur.*

No, **be** an entrepreneur, generating and communicating your ideas, **do** the business by running a pilot or creating a prototype then take steps to acquire the funding you need and you'll **have** what you need.

Letter from the Future

These instructions should be scanned quickly before you begin to write. If you don't plan to write the letter now, move on and return to this page when you're ready. Write it quickly without thinking about it, just putting down what comes first. Maximum writing time 10 minutes.

Write a letter to a friend dated 3 years from now but expressed as though it's the present...

"I'm sitting in my roof garden looking over the city/ I've just finished milking the goats... and thought I'd write..."

Imagine that your friend has not seen you during these 3 years and you have not had time to communicate regularly. You're giving an update on every aspect of your life: your business, your home, companions, family, finances, appearance and health, leisure pursuits and so on...

When it's finished, ask yourself:

- Are there any surprises?
- Which bits give me the biggest buzz?
- Does any of it seem completely 'pie-in-the-sky'?
- What would you be willing to give to make it real?

Anti-Saboteur Device

Major change is exciting and can be scary. When we begin to move out of our comfort zone we can, without being aware of it, sabotage our best intentions. Spot the saboteur by...

- Minding your language.
- Identifying and eliminating negative messages from yourself and others.
- Designing a reminder for yourself to prevent you from slipping back into old patterns: a slogan on the fridge door, something squeezy in your pocket, fairy lights round your desk that you switch on when the little voice says, "it'll never work"

SET OUT

You've got your vision. Now you need to do something about it. None of the above will make any difference if you don't actually begin. So write down 3 things you need to do to get started. Set a date to complete them and ask someone to hold you accountable – a friend, business partner, or a coach. It's not *their* responsibility of course; it just helps motivate you, knowing that you'll be asked to report progress!

If you were planning a holiday, you'd set a date, make a list of what you need to take, buy the guidebook and so on, but unless you actually set out, the holiday won't happen.

Some people love to dream about all the places they might go but they never actually go there. Some people don't like to be tied down and prefer to set out and go where the fancy takes them. But if you want to be sure of the holiday actually happening, you book. Advance booking equals money and time committed so, barring the unexpected, you'll be on that plane or driving off to your destination.

At least one of your 3 starter actions should be like that; an action that propels you forward. What could that be? Let's say it was advertising a product or an event. Before you do that, you need to have enough in place to ensure that you can deliver.

Notice I said 'enough' – not 'everything'. If you wait until everything is perfect, you'll never start at all. Move in as soon as the paint is dry! Some people are preparation freaks – cupboards full of beautiful stationery, pockets full of business cards but no actual business. Preparation is essential for action but don't let it be a substitute.

Your fresh horse is ready and waiting. You've packed your bag with your own Open Road resources, your excuse-demolisher, the gifts from past experience, and you're holding the Vision clearly before you.

If you want your Happy Ending to be a New Beginning, saddle up your horse and get going!

POST SCRIPT

Imagine the 'If Only' racing card. Running today in the 3.30 at Ayr, we have:

- I Could Do That
- You're Lucky
- I Always Meant To
- Chance Would Be A Fine Thing
- If Only

A friend of mine used to say that she hated going to the sort of parties where people were always whingeing about their unfinished novel.

"I wish they'd write the damn thing or shut up about it."

It's irritating to be on the receiving end of that sort of talk but it's seriously damaging if you're the one that's saying it.

Focusing on what you haven't got is a miserable state to be in and brings about more of the same.

Energy spent whingeing is energy wasted.

Sniping at others, even in the privacy of your own thoughts, poisons your attitude and is likely to affect how you behave towards them.

If someone else's life seems so good, why not give it a try? If you are always wishing you had taken another path, turn that wish into a vision, plan the journey, bury your dead horse and set out.

If you have good reasons not to, if you're really never going to do it, then THAT is *your* dead horse. Give it a decent burial; don't keep digging it up and mourning over it. Let go of the illusion that you're going to do things any differently.

So many people testify to the fact that tragedy or hardship awakens their appreciation for life and its 'ordinary' pleasures. Don't wait for such a wake-up call. Let go of the wishing, the envy, and the regrets and explore the life you've got.

ALISON CLARK

I am the classic serial self reinventor: secondary school teacher of English, playwright, retreat house leader, mother and owner of my consultancy, WORDS in ACTION. My home is in Scotland and my work takes me throughout the UK and beyond.

My most recent change is to move from the city of Glasgow, my home town, to the island of Bute in the Clyde estuary from where I work as writer, presenter and coach.

Photo - www.AndyWalters.co.uk

I have written for theatre, cabaret and stand-up comedy; for poetry magazines and newspapers. *How to Stop Flogging a Dead Horse* is my first published non-fiction book, the first of a series designed to ease readers through the whole gamut of transitions we face in our working and personal lives.

SUGGESTED RESOURCES

Here are some books and websites which I have found useful. I have included some well known classics because I continue to find them helpful.

Books

Stephen Covey, *The Seven Habits Of Highly Effective People*

Barbara Sher, *It's Only Too Late If You Don't Start Now*

Daniel Goleman, *Emotional Intelligence*

Spencer Johnson, *Who Moved My Cheese?*

Dr Richard Wiseman, *The Luck Factor*

Nicola Cairncross, *Money Gym: The Wealth Building Workout*

Anthony de Mello, *Awareness*

Annie Dillard, *Pilgrim at Tinker Creek*

Debbie Jenkins, Joe Gregory, *The Gorillas Want Bananas*

Websites

www.dti.gov.uk/er/

www.baxters.com

www.bgateway.com

www.go.uk.com

www.leanmarketing.co.uk

www.smallbusinessadvice.org.uk

www.wordsinaction.net